Your Towns and Cities in t

Chichester
in the Great War

Your Towns and Cities in the Great War

Chichester
in the Great War

John J. Eddleston

Pen & Sword
MILITARY

First published in Great Britain in 2016 by
PEN & SWORD MILITARY
an imprint of
Pen and Sword Books Ltd
47 Church Street
Barnsley
South Yorkshire S70 2AS

Copyright © John J. Eddleston, 2016

ISBN 978 1 78346 328 2

The right of John J. Eddleston to be identified as the author of this work has been asserted by him in accordance with the Copyright, Designs and Patents Act 1988.

A CIP record for this book is available from the British Library

All rights reserved. No part of this book may be reproduced or transmitted in any form or by any means, electronic or mechanical including photocopying, recording or by any information storage and retrieval system, without permission from the Publisher in writing.

Printed and bound in England
by CPI Group (UK) Ltd, Croydon, CR0 4YY

Typeset in Times New Roman by Chic Graphics

Pen & Sword Books Ltd incorporates the imprints of
Pen & Sword Archaeology, Atlas, Aviation, Battleground, Discovery, Family History, History, Maritime, Military, Naval, Politics, Railways, Select, Social History, Transport, True Crime, Claymore Press, Frontline Books, Leo Cooper, Praetorian Press, Remember When, Seaforth Publishing and Wharncliffe.

For a complete list of Pen and Sword titles please contact
Pen and Sword Books Limited
47 Church Street, Barnsley, South Yorkshire, S70 2AS, England
E-mail: enquiries@pen-and-sword.co.uk
Website: www.pen-and-sword.co.uk

Contents

    Introduction   7

1. An Ordinary Year – January to June 1914   9
2. The Early Days – September to December 1914   21
3. A War of Attrition – 1915   29
4. Naval Encounters and Other Battles – January to July 1916   43
5. The Somme – July to December 1916   53
6. The Royal Sussex Regiment   59
7. No End in Sight – January to April 1917   67
8. The Grinding Battle Continues – May to December 1917   71
9. No End in Sight – January to March 1918   81
10. The Great German Offensives – April to July 1918   85
11. The End – August to November 1918   89
12. Peace   93

    Index   99

Introduction

The city of Chichester has a long and distinguished history. An important Roman settlement it was known as Noviomagus Reginorum and was the capital of the Roman civitas in which it was situated. There was a direct connection to Londinium through the East Gate, a road known as Stane Street.

After the Roman departure from England, Chichester became an Anglo-Saxon settlement. It was captured by Aelle, the first King of the South Saxons, after which tribe the county of Sussex itself got its name. Aelle renamed the city in honour of his son Cissa, from which the modern place name is derived. Once again the town was a capital, this time of the Kingdom of the South Saxons. In the latter part of the ninth century, Chichester was fortified again by King Alfred of Wessex.

In 1066, after the Battle of Hastings, the Norman William I seized the English throne. At the time, the population of Chichester was around 1,500 souls. The town was then given to Roger de Montgomerie, the first Earl of Shrewsbury, for his part in the fighting at Battle and, soon afterwards, the castle was built. Later, however, the town became part of the estates of the Earl of Arundel and the castle formed the administrative centre of the western part of the Earl's estates. Chichester Cathedral was built in the late eleventh century and is dedicated to the Holy Trinity.

Amongst the famous people born in Chichester is William Huskisson, who served for some years as the local Member of Parliament but is more famous for being the first person to die as the consequence of a railway accident. Other people born in the city include actors Michael Elphick, Hugh Dennis, Patricia Routledge and Michael Wilding. It is also the birthplace of Body Shop founder, Anita Roddick.

During the Great War of 1914 to 1918 many of Chichester's sons answered the call to serve their country, including more than 100 men from the Shippam's meat paste factory. Over 300 of Chichester's men lost their lives in that terrible conflict. Many of their names are listed on the war memorial, which was originally erected in Eastgate Square but is now situated in Litten Gardens.

CHAPTER 1

An Ordinary Year – January to July 1914

The year 1914 dawned in Chichester – and indeed throughout the southern part of England – with a prolonged cold snap. In some places the temperature dropped to minus 16 but many people took advantage of this by skating on the frozen ponds and enjoying such winter sports as tobogganing down the frozen and snowy hills. That is not to say, however, that everyone in the town was happy and celebratory.

On Tuesday, 13 January, for instance, Ernest Porter appeared before the magistrates charged with a most serious offence. It was claimed that on the previous Saturday, 10 January, he had assaulted a 13-year-old-girl named Dowling. It transpired that, at around 5.15pm on that Saturday, Porter approached Constable Street and said that he wished to give himself up. When asked why, Porter replied, 'Well, I have pretty well strangled that little girl Dowling.' Porter was taken into custody and Constable Street then went to interview the girl in question and, of course, her parents.

When the girl told her story she explained that she had gone to Compton to fetch some milk for her mother, at around 3.30pm. As she was returning home to Up Marden she came to a bridge and it was there that Porter approached her and made a certain suggestion. Terrified, she shouted out for help but Porter seized her and stuffed a red handkerchief into her mouth. She struggled but he then took a white handkerchief from her basket and tied it tightly around her. She continued to struggle until he took a knife out of his pocket and said he would kill her. She then ceased to fight back, at which point he raped her.

On the second day of the magistrate's hearing, Porter himself was questioned and he admitted that the child's story was true in all respects, adding that he had been in a local public house when he saw her pass. He went after her with the full intention of doing what he did. He was then sent for trial at the next assizes.

Something of more cultural interest took place on 14 January when the mayor, Councillor Garland, and his wife held a ball at the Council House to celebrate his second year of office the previous November. Amongst the various entertainments was a piano recital by Miss Doris Glenn, who played some Chopin.

Another ball took place exactly one week later, on 21 January, but this time it was organised by a committee of the Sussex Yeomanry. This was an event that had first been instituted at the end of the Boer War. It had lapsed for a few years but was now revived. Apparently it was an excellent affair and thanks were given to the members who had organised the event: Sergeant Major Brown, Sergeant Baker, Lance Corporal Bartholemew and Troopers Howard, Harris, Lock and Petts.

A civil court case was heard on the same day as the Yeomanry Ball. Mr W.A. Trim, a cycle dealer of South Street, claimed the sum of one pound from Mrs Hall of Littlehampton. She had obtained a cycle from him but had neglected to pay for it, claiming that the instrument was defective. She told the court that her husband had used the bicycle to go to Worthing but had been unable to ride it back and had had to walk home. However, when Mr Trim pointed out that Mrs Hall had used the cycle for a full two weeks before making her complaint, the magistrates found in his favour and Mrs Hall was ordered to pay.

Four days after this, on 25 January, a most curious case was heard by the local magistrates. Two sailors, brothers Ernest and

Walter Dridge, were accused of breaking a window in the Royal Oak public house on 11 January. It seemed that the landlord of the Royal Oak, John Cobb, had previously given evidence against the brothers in a minor dispute and they now held a grudge against him. On the evening of the 10th they had been drinking in the Dolphin, which they left with a couple of bottles of beer. At around 12.20am on the 11th, John Cobb and his wife were woken by a tremendous smash and Mrs Cobb ran to the window where she saw two men in sailors' uniforms running into the house almost directly opposite, owned by the Dridge brothers. These two men were also seen by a live-in maid, Nellie Woods. There was also the fact that two broken beer bottles were found inside the Royal Oak and that these were positively identified by the landlord of the Dolphin as being identical to those he had sold to the two brothers. Despite all this very strong evidence, the magistrates, rather surprisingly, decided that the identification evidence was not strong enough and the charges were dismissed.

On 30 January, a meeting of the Chichester Guardians took place at which it was reported that the only district in the whole of West Sussex that showed an increase in the number of paupers in the local workhouse was Chichester. There was also a major problem with people begging on the streets and representations would be made to the police to stamp down on such activity. This policy seemed to be implemented rather quickly, for on 3 February, John Gallaghan was arrested for begging in North Street. He was discharged when he agreed to move on from the city.

On that same day, 3 February, a most exciting incident took place in the city centre. A horse belonging to Mr Field of Pound Farm bolted in The Hornet. It galloped off through the streets and eluded an attempt by Sergeant Beacher to stop it in East Street. It also managed to avoid a police constable near the Cross and was only stopped, finally, in West Street; but not before it had collided with a motor-cycle and sidecar.

On 10 February an inquest opened at the Royal West Sussex Hospital on the body of Seth Bridger, who worked for the

Chichester Gas Company and who lived at 15 Russell Street, Portfield. He died in the hospital on 6 February but he had been ill since a fall at work on 20 December 1913. His widow, Jane, gave evidence that he had told her that it was a bad fall, caused by some fault of his employers. He had felt ill ever since, with terrible pains in his side and had eventually been taken to hospital. The hearing was adjourned to give Seth's employers time to prepare their case. When it was resumed, on the 16th, the employers denied any responsibility and called medical experts who said that the injury could have been caused at any time. There were no witnesses to the accident having happened at Seth's work. A verdict of natural causes was returned.

A most saddening story was heard at another inquest, which also took place at the Royal West Sussex Hospital, on the very same day, 10 February. This hearing regarded a young child named William George Millyard, of 5 Cross Street, who had been badly burned on Saturday, 29 January.

The child's mother, Alice Maud Mary Millyard had gone out to visit a neighbour some time before 1.00pm on that fateful day, leaving the child with his father, who was asleep in a chair before the fire. A fireguard was secured in front of the roaring flames but William, who was apparently extremely fond of toast, had taken a slice of bread and a metal toasting fork and removed part of the guard. His father was woken from his slumbers by a terrible screaming. It seemed that the boy had dropped the bread and when he bent down to retrieve it his clothes had caught fire. He received extensive and deep burns to his right shoulder, his side and his chest. Rushed to hospital, he was cared for by Mr J.H.C. Green, the house surgeon but despite the best medical care William developed pneumonia and died on 5 February. A verdict of accidental death was returned.

Another minor case came before the magistrates on 16 February when Geoffrey Harn of The Globe pleaded guilty to driving a motor car at night, in South Street without lights. The policeman who stopped him was perhaps rather zealous in his work. Harn was driving without his lights switched on but the officer charged him with two offences; driving without front lights and driving without rear lights. Harn was fined 2/6d for each offence.

The local Licensing Committee sat to review licences on 14 February when complaints were made that there were far too many drinking establishments in the city of Chichester. Objections were made to the renewal of licences for: the Plough and Harrow in St Pancras; the Blacksmith's Arms in The Hornet; the Castle Inn, also in The Hornet; the Prince Arthur in Little London; the Good Intent in George Street; the Arundel Arms in Cavendish Street; and the Prince of Wales in Tower Street. The committee said it would look into each of these objections carefully.

On Wednesday 18 February an entertaining evening was organised by the staff and pupils of Chichester High School when a Kipling Medley took place. Stories and songs from the writer's works were performed; one of the high points was a gnome dance arranged by the principal, Miss Lane.

On 23 February, news of an air disaster hit the headlines of the local newspapers. A biplane aircraft crashed at West Wittering. Many local people were in the area, looking at the aerobatics being performed when suddenly the craft seemed to dive, oscillate from side to side and plunged into a field on Holme's Farm. The pilot, Ronald Kemp, was badly injured and taken to hospital in Chichester but his passenger, Mr E.T. Haynes, was killed.

Another tragedy was detailed in early March. On Sunday, 1 March, a 12-year-old girl, Letitia Cotton, was in Eastgate Street when she ran out into the road in front of a parked wagonette. She did not see a car, driven by Thomas Charles Warren of Southsea, who was driving through the city on his way to Arundel. He struck the child and immediately stopped. To his horror, when he got out of the vehicle to see how badly injured the girl was, he found that his rear wheel was still parked on her chest. Warren got back into the car and pulled forward a few feet but it was too late and Letitia died within a few minutes. At the subsequent inquest no blame was attached to Mr Warren, who claimed that he was only doing about ten miles an hour at the time of the impact. One of the witnesses called was none other than the Mayor, Councillor Garland, who claimed that in fact Warren was going too fast and estimated that his speed was closer to 35 miles per hour. Despite that testimony, a verdict of accidental death was returned.

On 20 March a local married couple, John and Annie Williams, appeared before the magistrates on a charge of being drunk and disorderly in West Street the previous day. They were arrested at 11.10pm by Constables Squires and MacKenzie and, having been found guilty, were fined. Since neither had the means to pay the fine, John ended up serving fourteen days imprisonment with hard labour, whilst his wife got seven.

The month ended on what could be described as a pleasant note. On 27 March, Chichester Cathedral was the venue for the Lenten concert when the Oratorio Society performed Verdi's Requiem. A very large audience attended the event and all the extra seating was occupied.

A terrible fatality occurred on 7 April when a 76-year-old naval pensioner, Henry Charles Kestall, was cut to pieces by a train at Nutbourne, a few miles west of Chichester. Henry was crossing the railway line when the 5.10pm express from Portsmouth Harbour to Brighton approached him at speed. Mr Kestall, who was quite deaf, heard neither the train, the train whistle or the shouts of Mrs Frances Leagus, who was close by. The unfortunate man was killed instantly and various body parts were later found scattered along the line.

It seemed that one particular Chichester constable was rather diligent in arresting people for travelling at night without lights. In the month of April, Constable Kenzie arrested Frank Philimore for riding a bicycle without a light at 10.25pm in West Street, Edith McCarthy for driving a motor car without lights in East Street and, most curiously, Walter Granger for riding a horse without a light at 11.50pm, also in West Street. Fines were imposed on all three miscreants.

On 11 April another court case publicised was that of a hawker named William Bradshaw who was charged with being drunk and disorderly the previous evening. What was significant about this case was that Bradshaw had used the foulest of language when being cautioned and had resisted arrest violently. Indeed, he was described by Sergeant Brett as the most violent and obstinate prisoner he had ever had to deal with. Bradshaw was sentenced to fourteen days hard labour.

20 April saw some amateur dramatics performed in Chichester, in aid of St Paul's Parish Fund. Two comedies, entitled *The Lady of Munster* and *The Sentinel* were well received by the audience.

On the last day of April, at the Lancastrian School in Chichester, prizes were awarded to pupils for regular attendance and good behaviour. Fifteen students received watches for five years' perfect attendance and eight more were given silver medals for three years' perfect attendance. Books were also awarded to those pupils who had a 97 per cent or better record over the past year.

On 6 May a meeting of influential local citizens took place to register their complaints about the state of Chichester station. The meeting was organised by the Mayor but was presided over by the Duke of Richmond and Gordon. Amongst the concerns discussed was the insufficiency of conveniences and the general state of the station, which had not been modernised since the early days of the railway. The platform was rather narrow and a large number of accidents had been recorded. The toilets were described as an absolute disgrace. In May 1913, one year ago now, the directors of the railway had been given a list of grievances and suggestions for improvements but nothing had been done. The chairman of the meeting assured the staff who worked at the railway station that no criticism was directed at them. It was decided to contact the directors again and point out that Chichester was a prestigious city and deserved a station that was fit for purpose.

The severity of some local laws was demonstrated on Monday 11 May when Charles Burt appeared before the magistrates and pleaded guilty to being a pedlar without a licence. He was sentenced to seven days imprisonment for the heinous crime of selling shoelaces door to door. However, the bench did show some mercy.

Burt was not in the best of health and the magistrates decided that he could serve his sentence in hospital, where he would receive the treatment he needed.

James Monkbar was not a very lucky man. He approached a gentleman in South Street and asked if he knew where he might get some work as a gardener. The gentleman replied that he did not know of anyone who might employ Monkbar, who then asked him if he might spare a few coppers. Unfortunately for Monkbar, the gentleman was Constable Stripp, who was in plain clothes and Monkbar found himself arrested for begging. Fortunately for him, he was let off with a caution as this was his first offence.

On Friday 22 May a severe thunderstorm blew into West Sussex from the Channel. There were reports of hailstones as large as walnuts falling in the Chichester area and, during the height of the storm, the Fire Brigade had to rush to Thomas Field's farm on the Bognor Road where a hayrick had been struck by lightning and set on fire. No sooner had they dealt with that incident than they were called to another farm where another rick had been set ablaze.

On the first day of June the annual Chichester Sports day was held at Priory Park. The weather was fine and the Chichester City Band provided music as the events took place. The meeting took five hours in all and the only hint of trouble during the day occurred when a gentleman named Palmer fell off his bicycle in a race. He escaped with a bruised elbow and was treated by the St John's Ambulance. In the evening the grounds of the park were illuminated and the City Band performed again.

On 13 June a performance of *Antigone* took place at the Bishop Otter College in the city. The large audience showed their appreciation of the event, which was described as 'most professional'. A few days later, on 18 June, Annie Williams was fined 2/6d for being drunk and disorderly in West Street at 6.00pm the previous evening.

For the first six months of the year 1914 the citizens of the ancient city of Chichester had gone about their business dealing with petty crime, organising entertainments, dealing with local issues and generally getting on with life. That June, however, saw an event take place in Bosnia that would change the lives of many of those same people, for on 28 June, shots rang out in Sarajevo that would reverberate across the world.

Many people believe that what was to become known as the Great War was started by the assassination of Archduke Franz Ferdinand and his wife Sophie by a Bosnian Serb, Gavrilo Princip. In fact, whilst this might well be described as the single event that precipitated war, the conditions for such a conflagration had been building over the previous years.

Germany, as a sovereign country, did not exist until 1871. What we now know as Germany was before then nothing more than a number of self-governing states, of which the most powerful was Prussia.

In 1866, war between Prussia and Austria saw a Prussian victory. Four years later, in 1870, another war, this time between Prussia and her German allies and France saw another victory for the Germanic state, as a consequence of which the territories of Alsace and Lorraine were ceded to Prussia. This massive increase in Prussian military prestige and importance led, under Bismarck, to the unification of the various states into the German Empire on 18 January 1871. On that date, the King of Prussia, Wilhelm I, became Emperor (or Kaiser) of the new Germany.

Kaiser Wilhelm I, the first emperor of a united Germany.

At this time, a number of European countries were considered to be great powers, of which Britain was the strongest. Other major powers were France, Russia, Italy, Austria-Hungary and the Ottoman Empire; but to this list had

Kaiser Wilhelm II, the German emperor whose imperial ambitions largely fuelled the march to war.

now to be added the newest super power, Germany. This addition led to disquiet and suspicion amongst the other powers. There was also the fact that Germany was now seeking new alliances to further increase her influence on the political scene.

In 1879 a treaty was signed between Germany and Austria-Hungary, agreeing mutual support if either were attacked. This treaty led to the French agreeing an alliance with Russia in 1892 and in 1904 the Entente Cordiale was signed between France and

Britain, although this was not a military alliance. Already, Europe was dividing into two opposing camps. In 1907, Russia joined Britain and France transforming the Entente Cordiale into a Triple Entente, although – again – it was not as firm a military commitment as that of Germany and Austria-Hungary.

Rivalries between the powers continued over the last years of the nineteenth and the first of the twentieth centuries. Increasingly these were focussed on the Balkans, where squabbling new or re-established nations were emerging from the declining Ottoman Empire. Jockeying for geopolitical advantage led to several wars of varying degrees of intensity involving, amongst others, Greece, Bulgaria, Serbia, Albania and Montenegro.

Serbia was keen to establish what she considered to be a historical kingdom of south Slavs. To do this she found herself particularly opposed by Austria-Hungary, which sought to quell unrest amongst its Slav population by extending its boundaries and thus keep Serbia at arm's length.

Archduke Franz Ferdinand and his wife just a few minutes before they were shot dead in Sarajevo, thus precipitating the Great War.

On the other hand, Russia considered herself the natural protector of the Slavs and, by extension, Serbia. Amongst the nationalist groups in Serbia, the most militant was the Black Hand. Whatever the realities of the plot, the first attempt to assassinate Archduke Franz Ferdinand (the heir to the aged Emperor Franz Joseph) during a visit to Sarajevo failed. Gavrilo Princip seized an opportunity to act later on that day and, with two shots, fatally wounded both the Archduke and his wife Sophie.

From this point the complexities of the Balkans question became enmeshed in the European alliance system, the result of which was that by the end of the first week of August most of the major powers in Europe were at war.

CHAPTER 2

The Early Days – September to December 1914

When war was declared the people of Chichester soon showed their support for the conflict. As early as 1 September, a meeting of the Chichester City Aid Society took place at Langley House in West Street, the home of Admiral and Mrs Holland. The Mayoress, Mrs Garland, made a speech thanking all those citizens who had donated items so far. She went on to say that over 4,600 items had been given including medical supplies and clothing.

The very next day, 2 September, another meeting was held. This time it was the farmers of Sussex who met at the Corn Exchange to hear a speech detailing the most suitable crops to grow and how best those crops might be fertilised in order to optimise production for the duration of the fighting.

At the outbreak of war the various divisions of the regular army were sent to France as the BEF or British Expeditionary Force. Its first famous battle was that at Mons after which the BEF fought a retreat to the Marne. It was during this very early period of the war that the first men from Chichester fell.

The first four deaths of local men were all from the Royal Sussex Regiment. Regimental Sergeant Major William Cleare, who had lived at 54 York Road, was killed in action fighting the Germans at Priez on 10 September. On the same day, Private Charles Wheeler, of 3 Westhampnett Road, died of wounds he had suffered. Four days later, on 14 September, Private Dennis Sydney Hilton and Private Albert Thomas Yeatman were both killed in action at the hamlet of Troyon, north of Vendresse.

In the first weeks of September hundreds of young men gathered at Chichester barracks to enlist in the army. The men waiting in the long queue were able to watch those who had already been accepted being drilled on the parade ground. The majority of the men there had never even been to Chichester before.

Two more local men were to die in the next few days, though neither was in the Royal Sussex. On 16 September, Archibald Reginald White of the 11th Hussars died from wounds inflicted whilst fighting at the Marne, On 17 September, the same battle claimed the life of John Garside Fogden, King's Royal Rifle Corps. John lived at 2 Washington Street with his wife, Florence. Already six Chichester families were in mourning.

On 22 September 1914, three British cruisers were patrolling the North Sea when they were encountered by a German submarine, the U9. The first ship, HMS *Aboukir* was torpedoed and sank within twenty minutes, with the loss of 527 men. The captains of the other two ships, HMS *Cressy* and HMS *Hogue,* thought that the first ship had struck a mine and so were unaware that there was a submarine in the vicinity. They went to pick up survivors and the U9 launched two more torpedoes at HMS *Hogue* which also sank. Soon afterwards, the *Cressy* was also attacked and sunk. In a little over two hours, Britain had lost three cruisers and over 1,400 men. One of the men serving on the *Hogue* was Able Seaman Charles William Ansell of Birdham Locks to the south of Chichester. He was the first naval casualty of the war from the city.

On 23 September it was reported that a number of retired police officers had rejoined the West Sussex Constabulary to replace reservists who had been called up. In Chichester itself these men included Sergeant Beacher and Constables Grender, Heffer, Wilkins,

HMS Hogue, *on which Charles William Ansell became the first naval casualty of war from the Chichester region.*

Riddett, Tuckey, King and Fry. Other men, including William Clark, Alfred Watts and Victor Weston, were sworn in as Special Constables.

One more local man was to be killed in action in the month of September. Also serving in the Royal Sussex Regiment, he was Private Leonard Irish, of 14 The Hornet, who was killed on 29 September. He was mourned by his parents, Walter and Fanny Irish.

On 3 October, an application was heard from the Chief Constable that in view of the large number of men who would be stationed at Chichester, the sale of intoxicating liquor at all venues should henceforth be stopped at 10.00pm. The application was granted and came into force on Thursday, 8 October.

Also in October a small toy making industry was established in the city. To date eleven women and girls were employed doing needlework at Ivy Bank, in St John's Street, making shirts and socks for the soldiers at the front. These ladies now became engaged in making small toys for the people of Chichester to buy as Christmas presents for their children. The funds raised would be used to purchase more material and equipment so that more clothing could be made for the soldiers.

On 28 October, Margaret Willshire appeared before the magistrates charged with the forgery of a cheque for £1 12s, supposedly from a Captain Lancaster. Margaret, who was a domestic servant, had gone to Mr Heather's fruit shop and asked him to cash the cheque for her. Mr Heather knew Captain Lancaster, so readily cashed the cheque, only later realising that Margaret's signature on the back was in the same hand as the writing on the cheque itself.

Immediately, Mr Heather sent one of his employees, William Buler, out to find the woman and he saw Margaret outside a shop in South Street. He then escorted her back to the fruit shop, where she was arrested by Sergeant Evans. It transpired that Margaret worked as a maid for Captain Lancaster and when he was interviewed he confirmed that he had not written out the cheque. The magistrates decided that this was an offence too serious for them to deal with and Margaret was sent for trial at the next Lewes assizes.

During this month, four more men from Chichester gave their lives for their country. All four were killed in action, the first being Frank Feast of the East Surrey Regiment, who lived at 44 Tower Street with his wife, Dorothy. He was killed on 14 October. On the same day, Private Ernest Walker of the Middlesex Regiment was killed. Two lance corporals were the last to die in this month. The first was George Burnett of the Coldstream Guards. He lived at 105

St Pancras and was killed on 29 October. The very next day, Lance Corporal Francis Hurst was killed in an action at Shrewsbury Forest, near Ypres.

November was a bloody month for the men of Chichester, with no less than seven men from the city losing their lives. Four of these were from the army, including Captain Arthur Frederic Skaife of the Middlesex Regiment who was killed on 1 November. He was the son of Frederick and Josephine Skaife, who lived at North Street House, 57 North Street, Chichester. In fact, Mr and Mrs Skaife were under the impression that they had lost both their sons to the war. They had already received notice that their youngest son, Captain Eric Skaife, had been killed in action on 19 October but in November they received a letter from him stating that he had been wounded but was now a prisoner of war and was being well looked after in Germany.

The other three casualties in November were naval personnel.

North Street, Chichester.

Another view of North Street.

HMS *Good Hope* was a cruiser, which left Portsmouth on 2 August, bound for North America, where she would act as a reinforcement to Rear Admiral Craddock's force. Later she was sent down to the Falkland Islands, where she stayed until 22 October and then steamed, via Cape Horn, for the west coast of South America. On 1 November, *Good Hope*, along with a second cruiser, HMS *Monmouth*, met the German cruisers *Scharnhorst* and *Gneisenau* at Coronel, off the coast of Chile. Both the British ships were sunk and there were no survivors. Amongst the dead was Leading Stoker James John Hellyer, a native of Somerstown, who died aboard the *Good Hope*.

The other two sailors who died in November both perished on 26 November on the same ship. HMS *Bulwark* was a battleship ordered to patrol the English Channel on the lookout for German ships. On 26 November she was anchored off Sheerness in Kent when an internal explosion ripped her apart. A total of 736 men were killed, including Stoker 2nd Class Edward John Cotton, of 2 Lion Street, and Able Seaman Albert John Freeman, of 52 Oving Road, Portfield.

On 2 December the mayor and mayoress announced that they would organize a treat for the dependants of the men from Chichester who had enlisted in the forces. They expected the number of guests to number around 1,000 and therefore would hold the event at the Olympic skating rink. The event would consist of tea and other refreshments and would be followed by entertainment. It would take place on Christmas Day and they now appealed for helpers and donations.

There was another treat on Christmas Day; but this was for the inmates of the workhouse. In the morning there was a service in the chapel, followed at 12.30 by Christmas dinner in the hall, which the chairman and members of the board attended. The meal consisted of roast beef, roast pork, mutton, vegetables and Yorkshire pudding and was followed by plum pudding. Finally, at 6.00pm, the inmates were treated to a musical concert in the hall.

December, thankfully, saw no more men from Chichester perish in the war. However, the first few months of fighting had seen nineteen Chichester men, fifteen from the army and four from the navy, killed in the defence of their country.

CHAPTER 3

A War of Attrition – 1915

When the war originally broke out, many people believed that it would be over by Christmas. By the beginning of 1915, however, it was clear to most people that this would be a long, bloody and difficult war. That was certainly true for the authorities and the logistics required for fighting and winning such a war were now becoming abundantly clear.

Perhaps one single news item can illustrate the planning needed to maintain the war effort. In January 1915, the War Office announced that they needed 200,000 fresh, new-laid eggs a week to feed the wounded soldiers and sailors in hospitals at home and at the front. It was for this reason that Mrs Close opened the Egg Depot at 57 East Street in Chichester on 20 January. Mrs Close and her committee then requested one dozen eggs should be donated each week from each village and hamlet in the surrounding area. Individuals were also asked to donate. The depot was open from 10.00am to 3.30pm each day and the War Office agreed to cover the costs of carriage from Chichester. The eggs were sent on by train at 5.14pm each Wednesday. In the first week 336 eggs were sent and by the second week of operation this had risen to 744.

Meanwhile, there was news of another naval disaster. On 15 January, whilst she was on patrol, HMS *Viknor* hit a mine off the

East Street in Chichester, where the egg depot was situated.

coast of Ireland and sank with the loss of all the men on board. One of those men was Private Arthur Bridle of the Royal Marine Light Infantry. He was a Chichester man and lived at 3 Franklin Place.

The people of Chichester were certainly helping the war effort. On 27 January another appeal was made through the local newspapers. This time the request was for tobacco, cigarettes, fruit and other comforts for the wounded men who were being treated in hospitals in the city.

An event which originally was largely ignored by the local newspapers but would later prove to be highly significant, took place in early February. On 4 February, the German authorities declared that they would now consider the waters around Great Britain to be a war zone. From that date onwards German submarines would attack all shipping around the British Isles. It was a decision that would have far reaching consequences in the future.

In mid-February, Frederick John Collins Adams, who had served as the Chief Clerk in the Office of Surveyor of Taxes in Chichester for thirty-three years, died. He was only 56 years old and his obituary thanked him for his loyal service to the city. No such

One of the recruitment posters used by the government to persuade Britons to join the army.

The Germans also had recruitment posters.

obituary was published a few days later when Second Lieutenant David Yorke, a Chichester man, was killed in action at Ypres on 17 February.

In March, the War Office took over the Graylingwell Hospital. It was expected that the hospital would deal with around 1,000 wounded men by the following month. Dr H.A. Kidd, the medical superintendent at Graylingwell, was appointed to take charge of the facility and was given the rank of lieutenant colonel. All the hospital staff were retrained to cope with the sort of injuries that they would soon have to deal with.

On 10 March, the British launched an attack at Neuve Chapelle, a conflict that would last just three days. That short time cost the

Graylingwell Hospital, where so many wounded soldiers were treated.

lives of 7,000 British soldiers. Poor communications, and the very inadequate availability of artillery meant that the initial promising start came to nothing. All those lives had been lost for very little gain.

On the 12th of the month another local man made the ultimate sacrifice for his country. Rifleman Joseph Percy Penfold, the son of Albert and Annie Penfold, of 2 Babington Villa, Broadway, Summersdale, died of wounds received at the front line. Joseph was just 18 when he died.

On 15 April, the Women's Emergency Corps held a meeting in the home of Mr and Mrs Henty in Oaklands Park. The meeting was chaired by Lady Talbot, the wife of the local Member of Parliament, and its aim was to support the wives and children of the men who were away fighting in the war. It also sought to help in finding employment for women who were thrown out of work. It was decided that a register would be set up to list those women who were capable of working and could, perhaps, turn their hands to anything.

On 22 April, the Second Battle of Ypres opened. At the start of this battle the Germans made the first use of chlorine gas in significant quantities on the Western Front. Later in the year in July at Hooge, near Ypres, the Germans used another new weapon, flame-throwers, for the first time against the British.

Three days after Second Ypres began, on 25 April, the Allies landed troops on the Gallipoli peninsula. It would turn out to be a campaign that would eventually cost the Allies a quarter of a million casualties and would, in large part, be an example of how not to conduct an amphibious campaign.

May brought an incident that would have extremely far-reaching effects. On the first day of the month the RMS *Lusitania* set sail from New York, bound for Liverpool. At 2.10pm on 7 May she was off the coast of Ireland when she encountered a German submarine, the U20. The submarine fired a torpedo which struck the *Lusitania* close to her bow. Another explosion, from within the ship, caused it to sink rapidly and it went down with the loss of 1,195 lives, 128 of whom were American; that fact caused massive outrage in the

The landings at Gallipoli; note the ships in the background.

The Lusitania, *the sinking of which hardened American opinion against the Central Powers.*

How the New York Times *reported the loss of the* Lusitania.

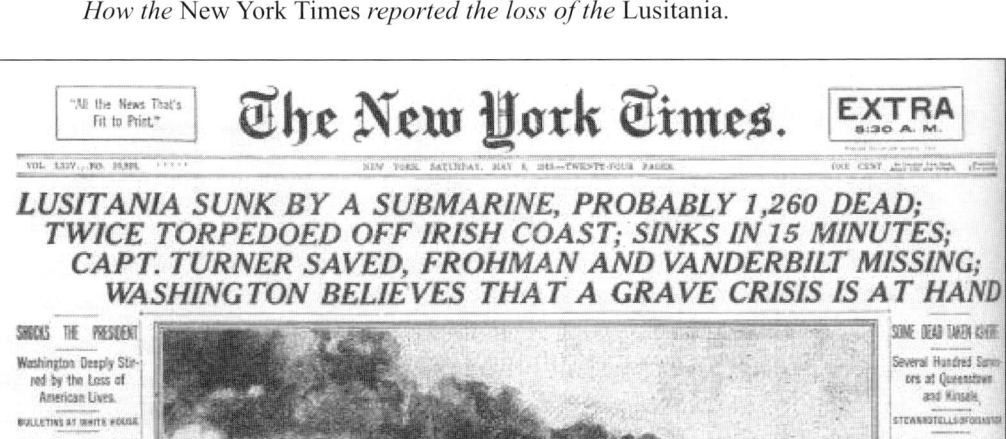

United States and went some way to changing the attitude of the American people towards involvement in the war.

May was a terrible month for some families in Chichester, for the list of local men killed in France and Belgium was a long one. The first death to be recorded was that of Lance Corporal Alan James Lee, of 32 St James' Road, Portfield. He was killed in action on 8 May.

Much worse was to follow the next day. The British had decided to attack the German lines at Aubers Ridge as part of a combined Franco-British offensive. The result was a complete disaster for the British, with over 11,000 casualties on the first day. On that day, no fewer than eight Chichester men were killed at Richebourg l'Avoué. These men, all from the Royal Sussex Regiment, were: Private Douglas Arthur, of 6 Parchment Street; Private Wyndham Carver; Private George James Harper, of 4 East Walls; Private William Morris, of 37 Tower Street; Private George Rossiter, of 22 St Pancras; Lance Corporal Edward Henry Bennett, of 21 St James' Road, Portfield; Lance Corporal Thomas Richard Bull, of 118 St Pancras; and Corporal William John Reeves Somers, of George Street. A ninth Chichester man, Private Thomas Longlands of 13 St James' Road, Portfield was wounded and died from those wounds the following day, 10 May.

On 12 May, the first batch of wounded soldiers bound for Graylingwell arrived at Chichester Station. The intake consisted of 150 men, one third of whom were stretcher cases. Despite the short notice, their transport to the hospital ran smoothly and all the men were soon receiving the best medical treatment available.

In June it was announced that the annual Goodwood Race Meeting, due to take place in July, had been postponed by the Duke of Richmond because of the war. It was also in June that Edwin and Minnie Turner, of 27 South Street and who were the parents of Arthur Morris Turner, were informed that their son had been killed in action in the Dardenelles. Arthur, who was just 22, had migrated to New Zealand a few years before the outbreak of hostilities. As soon as war broke out he had joined the New Zealand Army and

Men of the Royal Sussex Regiment, marching to war through the streets of Chichester.

had been amongst the first troops to be sent to fight in Europe. He was just one of over 8,000 New Zealand troops killed or wounded in the fiasco that was the Gallipoli campaign.

Reports were published in June that many of the wounded soldiers from Graylingwell were being taken for trips into the surrounding countryside for convalescence purposes. They visited such places as Slindon, Arundel, Eartham and Aldwick and some were taken to Dale Park. Others were invited to Goodwood House, where they were treated to tea by the Duke of Richmond. Many local families in Chichester were also kind enough to invite soldiers into their homes.

On 23 June, Alexandra Day was marked in the city by a number of fundraising events, including a sale of roses to raise funds for the Royal West Sussex Hospital. There was also a large jumble sale at the Olympia skating rink, where the admission was 2d. The roses sale alone raised over £100.

At the end of the month some errant parents were summoned to court to explain why they had not been sending their children to school. One such miscreant was William Harrison who explained that he simply could not control his ten-year-old son George. William told the magistrates that he had cajoled the boy and even given him a number of sound thrashings, but all to no avail. The Chairman of the Bench suggested that the thrashings administered were not severe enough.

On Monday, 5 July, a gentleman named Albert Wright appeared

South Street, Chichester.

in court charged with setting fire to a hay rick, an offence to which he pleaded guilty. It appeared that Albert found life difficult in normal society and preferred to be looked after in prison. He had previously been sentenced to terms of eight years, three years and five years in prison for similar offences. Within days of being released from jail, Albert would simply repeat the offence so that he could be taken back into custody and looked after. He was successful on this occasion too, being sentenced to another seven years.

Two days later, on 7 July, a most violent gale swept through southern England and many trees were blown down in the Chichester area. Towards the end of the month, the local newspapers informed readers that the Reverend Father McFayden, of St Richards' Roman Catholic Church, had been badly injured in Brighton. Father McFayden was riding a motor-cycle when he collided with another vehicle at a corner. He was admitted to the Sussex County Hospital with a fracture at the base of his skull.

Later in the month, the first anniversary of the war was marked with a public meeting in Eastgate Square. The meeting was very well attended and began with the singing of the hymn *O God our help in ages past*. A number of speeches followed and the meeting ended with the singing of the National Anthem.

The details of more local casualties were published. Five more Chichester men were killed in August, including two, Sapper John James Johnson, of 22 Chapel Road and Sapper Arthur Henry Piggott, of 24 Westhampnett Road, who died on the same day, 9 August.

In September the 4th Royal Sussex were in action in the Dardanelles and many men were wounded. One local man, Private William Tabour, was sent to Graylingwell to recover. Two more, Private Ernest Tabour, the brother of William, and Private Sidney Smith, were in hospital at Eastleigh.

It was also early in September that Joe Grainger appeared in court charged with assaulting John Hawkes, the landlord of the Castle Inn, situated on The Hornet. Apparently Grainger owed John the sum of five shillings and when asked to repay it said that he would do so if John came to his home to collect it. The two men walked down Whyke Lane towards Grainger's house, John holding the hand of his eight-year-old daughter, who had asked if she might come with him. Suddenly, Grainger turned and struck John Hawkes in the face. The blow was so severe that Hawkes fell to the ground, taking his daughter with him. John lost two teeth and his daughter sustained bruising to her face and arms. For this brutal attack Grainger received the rather lenient sentence of one month's imprisonment with hard labour.

In mid-September, Mrs Bonner, of 20 Bognor Road, received a letter from her son, William, who was serving in Gallipoli. In that letter he told a tale of a remarkable escape from death.

On 28 June, he and his comrades were attacking the Turks when a bullet struck him in the upper thigh. The bullet hit his purse, which was in his pocket at the time, bounced upwards and then hit the spare ammunition he was carrying, setting it alight. Thinking quickly, William took off his blazing tunic and threw it to one side. Checking his purse he found that the bullet had struck a penny, which was now badly bent. The only injury William suffered was a minor scratch to his stomach.

On 25 September, the Battle of Loos opened in France. It was significant for the first use of poison gas by the British. Many British lives were lost before the campaign ended on 8 October and such was the outcry over the size of the British losses and the handling of reserves that the commander of the British Expeditionary Force, Sir John French, would lose much of his support.

In this month, five more of Chichester's sons gave their lives for their country, four of them at the Battle of Loos. One of these was Sergeant Archibald Thomas Cleare, of 54 York Road. He was the brother of RSM William Cleare, who had been one of the very first casualties, killed on 10 September, 1914. Archibald was killed on 25 September on the opening day of the offensive.

It was not until October that Mr and Mrs Cleare were told of the death of their second son, Archibald. This one family had already given much to the war effort, for a third son, Sergeant F.A. Cleare,

Sir John French, the original commander of the British Expeditionary Force, who lost his command in December 1915, amongst other things, for his handling of the Battle of Loos.

was also serving and was now in hospital in Birmingham, recovering from a bullet in his leg.

On 29 October, a solemn service of remembrance took place in Chichester Cathedral. The service was in memory of Edith Cavell, an English nurse who had been working in Belgium. She treated wounded soldiers from both sides, without distinction, but helped around 200 Allied soldiers to escape from the country. For that offence she was arrested, put on trial for treason and sentenced to death. She was shot at 7.00am on 12 October, her death causing outrage not just in Britain but throughout the world.

On Monday, 1 November, new postal charges were brought into effect. Letters up to one ounce would now cost 1d and letters up to two ounces, 2d. At about the same time, the parents of Corporal A.W. Norman, of 17 St John Street, were informed that their son had been wounded the very first time he had gone into action and was now a prisoner in Prussia.

The news was not so good for Kate Vick, of 2 Ettrick Road, who was informed that her son, Lance Corporal Bernard Charles Vick, was in charge of a bombing party that had gone towards the German lines on 14 October. None of the party had been seen since and they were all listed as missing in action. Later in the year Mrs Vick would be informed that her son was dead.

On 12 November, 74 year old George Keates was laid to rest in Chichester Cemetery. George had served 26 years in the police force and now had five sons serving in the army. Only two of those sons had been able to obtain leave to attend the funeral, Corporal Alfred Charles Keates and Private Arthur Keates, both of who had been awarded the Queen's Medal.

On Monday 15 November a curious incident took place in the centre of Chichester. A horse attached to a delivery van of the Chichester Steam Laundry bolted in The Hornet. It galloped along East Street and at The Cross dashed into South Street. The turn being rather severe, the horse then crashed through the window of W.H. Barrett's, a stationers' shop. The van remained on the street whilst the badly cut horse stood inside the shop. Fortunately the horse survived and the only human injury was suffered by Mr E.H. Thompson, a customer in the shop at the time. He received some minor cuts from flying glass.

On 8 December, 65 year old Rosie Noyce, of 42 Oving Road, appeared in court charged with stealing a piece of bacon worth 2/6d from Kimbell and Sons of East Street on 3 December. Apparently Mrs Noyce placed a slice of bacon underneath her coat whilst the shop was crowded but she was seen by another customer, Emma Saunders, who reported the matter to the proprietor, David Kimbell. He followed Mrs Noyce out of the shop and signalled to a nearby constable, who arrested Mrs Noyce and took her back to the shop, where the slice of bacon was discovered. For this offence Rosie was fined £1 and ordered to pay that amount at one shilling a week.

Four more men from the city were killed in the last two months of 1915, one of whom was Private Henry Leonard James Penfold, of 30 Adelaide Road. He was wounded near Loos on 8 November and succumbed to his injuries on 15 November.

In all, forty of Chichester's sons had fallen in 1915. Much worse was to come the following year.

CHAPTER 4

Naval Encounters and Other Battles – January to July 1916

The year 1916 began in Chichester with a prosecution for cruelty. Henry Blunden, a gamekeeper, and his son Charles were found guilty of four cases of cruelty to dogs. Their trial, which took place on 8 January, detailed how two spaniels and two retrievers were found to be little more than bags of bones. The dogs actually belonged to a Mr Bevis, who had left the animals with Blunden after joining the army.

At about the same time a door to door collection took place in Chichester for the Red Cross. It raised the sum of £12 9s. Some of the money was also earmarked for an Italian Relief Fund.

On 18 January, some films were shown at Graylingwell Hospital to entertain the injured troops recovering there. In addition to the films, Miss Peacock played the piano and Mr Moss played the banjo. One of the final pieces was a comedy sketch, *The Broken Mirror*, performed by two of the patients and an orderly.

This terrible war had now been raging for almost sixteen months. The slaughter of men in the trenches on the Western Front and in other theatres of war meant that the government had to face the mounting demand for men. It was this knowledge that led to the passing of the Military Service Act. It was to receive Royal Assent on 27 January and would mean that men within set age limits could be conscripted into the forces. This was why, on the 24th of the month, Alderman Garland, the Mayor, appealed for all able-bodied men, especially those who were single, to join the forces before the Act came into effect. In order to facilitate recruitment, the office at the Council House would remain open between 6.00pm and 7.00pm each evening.

February opened with a grand gift sale at the Cattle Market, which raised the princely sum of £1,150 for the Red Cross and for local farmers who had been ruined owing to shortage of labour. On the 12th of the month, Thomas Harris was charged with being drunk in Broyle Road. He had been arrested by Constable Ellis who had, until recently, served in France until he was wounded. Invalided out of the army, he rejoined the police in time to arrest Harris, who was fined five shillings.

The first Chichester soldier to be killed in 1916 died on Valentine's Day, 14 February. Private Ernest James Bridger of the Royal Sussex Regiment was killed at Hooge on that day. He was the son of Ernest and Sarah Bridger, of 3 Russell Street.

On 1 March Chichester's Post Office announced that it was cutting its opening times. From now on it would only open from 9.00am to 1.00pm and then from 2.00pm to 7.00pm. However, telegrams could still be sent between 1.00pm and 2.00pm by taking them to a side entrance, where they could be handed in.

The Military Service Act was now law and men were now subject to conscription. When men were called to serve they could appeal on various grounds and in Chichester one of the first to appeal was a local tax collector. In fact it was his employer who put the appeal in, stating that there had at one time been four collectors in the city but three had already joined the army. One had already been killed and another been badly wounded at Loos and had lost an arm. There was, at the present time, no one else trained to do the job, though a young lady had been taken on but needed to be trained.

An exemption was given for one month so that the lady's training could be completed.

On 17 March, the first men who had failed to answer their call-up appeared before the magistrates at Chichester. There were seven men in the dock: Henry George; brothers Alfred, Frederick and Frank Hill; Wilfred Tee; and brothers Morris and Frederick Lee. Each man was fined forty shillings for failing to report and they were all then handed over to a military escort, who took them to the barracks. Two of those eight men would later be killed in action.

April saw four more Chichester men killed in action in France. All were men of the Royal Sussex Regiment and three of them died in the Loos sector. The highest ranking was Second Lieutenant Terence Fitzsimons, who was killed on 4 April.

A strange civil case was heard in the Chichester County Court on 19 April when Mrs Stair attempted to sue Mr Wren for the sum of £1. Mrs Stair claimed that she was in Chichester at 9.25 pm on 26 February. It had been snowing and the pavements were covered in deep snow. Rather than risk falling over, Mrs Stair had been walking in a pathway cleared in the road by a snowplough. A vehicle driven by Mr Stair clipped her and knocked her over and her coat was damaged. The judge found in favour of Mrs Stair but when he discovered that the coat in question was two years old, he reduced the damages to just ten shillings.

24 April was Easter Monday that year; it saw fighting much closer to home, for it was on that day that armed men and women of the Irish Volunteers revolted in Dublin and other Irish towns in what would become known as the Easter Rising. The rebellion against British Rule would last for six days and during that period, sixty-four Irish Volunteers, 132 British troops and Irish police and 254 civilians were killed. The revolt would later lead to the execution of sixteen rebels.

May was a tragic one for many families in Chichester. Until almost the end of the month three soldiers had lost their lives. Arguably the saddest of these was the death of Private William Burrell. William was one of the two sons of Charles and Fanny

Burrell of Mill House, Fishbourne. He enlisted in November 1914; but soon after arriving in France he went missing. After some weeks he was caught, put on trial and sentenced to death, but this was commuted to imprisonment. When he was released William was sent back to his regiment, the Royal Sussex, which was fighting at Loos and soon he went absent for a second time. Captured again he was tried and sentenced to death for a second time; but this time the dread sentence was carried out and William was shot on 22 May. What makes the story even sadder is that his brother, Ernest, had been killed near Ypres on 6 March. Within three months Charles and Fanny Burrell lost both of their sons.

On Saturday, 27 May, Mrs Frances Bird was summoned to court on a charge of assaulting a teacher, Thomas Hornby, on 12 May. The case arose because, under Section 122 of the Children's Act of 1908, the local authority had the power to examine children they believed to be verminous. A Doctor Smedley had given Mr Hornby permission to peform such examinations on the children in his care and one of those charges was Mrs Bird's daughter, who was found to be carrying lice.

The child was sent home, whereupon Mrs Bird went to the school, walked into Mr Hornby's class and struck him after using foul language. She also tried to strike Mrs Hornby, who was a classroom assistant, and finally had to be forcibly removed from the premises; but no sooner was Mrs Bird off school premises than she picked up a stone and threw it through one of the windows, striking Mr Hornby in the cheek. Found guilty of assault, Mrs Bird was fined fifteen shillings and costs.

The last day of May was a most terrible day for the citizens of Chichester. On 31 May the long awaited great sea battle between the British and Germans took place.

Since the war began the British had been blockading German ports and this was an attempt to break the blockade. It was on 31 May that no less than 151 British ships met with ninety-nine ships from the German navy, at Jutland. The battle raged into June during which the Germans lost eleven ships and 2,551 men killed. The

Another British poster, calling for naval volunteers. Notice the pay, at 1/3d per day.

British lost fourteen ships and 6,094 men. Both sides claimed victory but in effect the battle achieved British aims, as the blockade of German ports was maintained and the German High Seas Fleet remained, effectively, in harbour until the end of the war.

For the people of Chichester, the loss of four of those ships – HMS *Black Prince*, HMS *Invincible*, HMS *Indefatigable* and HMS *Queen Mary,* was especially significant, for on each of those ships men from Chichester died.

HMS *Black Prince* was an armoured cruiser and she was hit by at least eight heavy shells. She sank within fifteen minutes and there were no survivors amongst her crew of 857. Amongst her dead were Henry Cecil Applin, Alfred John Ayling, Harold Arthur Jupp and Frederick William May, all men from Chichester.

The other three ships were all battlecruisers. HMS *Queen Mary* broke in two when a shell hit the forward magazine. There were only eighteen survivors from the ship and 1,266 men were killed. Included in the latter figure were two men from Chichester, George Oliver Pratt and William Turner.

HMS *Invincible* was also destroyed when a shell hit one of her magazines. Only six men survived the subsequent explosion and amongst the 1,026 men killed were seven Chichester men. They were Bertie Charles Arnell, James Edward Bailey, Herbert John Bennett, George Greedus, Arthur John Hall, Edward George Henry Mills and 17-year-old Jack Smith.

The last of these four ships, HMS *Indefatigable*, was badly damaged and began sinking and listing to port when she was hit again. Only two men out of her complement of 1,019 survived. Amongst the dead was Alan Broadbridge, a Chichester man who lived at 30 Whyke Lane. His death brought the dreadful toll up to fourteen men; but it could have been far worse, for initial reports on the battle in the *Chichester Observer* stated that as many as eighty Chichester men might have been killed.

In June, another naval tragedy effected Chichester. At the beginning of the month, Field Marshal Earl Kitchener sailed to visit Russia to discuss military matters with the Tsar and his government. HMS *Hampshire* had taken part in the Battle of Jutland and had returned safely to its base at Scapa Flow. On 5 June the ship set sail for Russia with Kitchener and his staff on board. The weather was appalling and the captain of the ship decided that it would be better

HMS Black Prince, *lost at Jutland with four Chichester men on board.*

HMS Queen Mary *at Jutland. Two Chichester men were listed amongst the dead.*

HMS Indefatigable, *also lost at Jutland with one Chichester man, Alan Broadbridge, on board.*

to return to port. The *Hampshire* was only one and a half miles from shore when a massive explosion ripped her apart. The ship had hit a German mine and sank within fifteen minutes. More than 600 men were killed, including Earl Kitchener; amongst the dead were three from Chichester: Able Seaman William Arthur Freeman; and Stokers 1st Class Charles George Joseph Ayling and Harry Noel. The loss was a second tragedy for Richard and Fanny Freeman, of 52 Oving Road, Portfield as this was the second son they had lost in the war. William Freeman's brother, Albert, was killed on 26 November 1914 when HMS *Bulwark* blew up.

On Sunday 16 June, a memorial service took place in Chichester Cathedral for the seventeen local men who perished in the Battle of Jutland and the sinking of HMS *Hampshire*. There was standing room only inside the Cathedral. Amongst the congregation were 150 wounded soldiers from Graylingwell and the Royal West Sussex Hospital.

At the end of June, more Chichester soldiers lost their lives. A major offensive was to open at about the same time as the Somme.

High Command decided that in order to divert the Germans as to where this would take place, a diversionary attack should be launched against the German lines at Richebourg l'Avoué. Known popularly as the Battle of the Boar's Head, the attack took place on 30 June and involved three battalions of the Royal Sussex Regiment.

Fighting bravely under very heavy fire, the men succeeded in seizing the German front line and held it for some hours before being forced to retreat to their own lines. In five hours of fighting, seventeen officers and 349 men were killed and over 1,000 were either wounded or taken prisoner. The day was described in the regimental history as 'The Day Sussex Died'. Five of those who perished in this diversion were from Chichester. The following day the planned major offensive opened at a place whose name would go down in history as a catastrophic day for the British army. On 1 July, the Battle of the Somme began.

CHAPTER 5

The Somme – July to December 1916

The Battle of the Somme lasted until 18 November 1916 and was, at least in part, an attempt to relieve pressure on the French at Verdun and to draw German forces away from that part of the front. It was the bloodiest battle on the Western Front in the Great War. On the very first day Britain suffered just under 60,000 casualties, of whom one third were killed.

In fact the Somme was not just one large continuous battle. The campaign was divided into phases and amongst the actions that made up the Somme campaign was Albert, Fromelles, Delville Wood, Pozières Ridge, Flers-Courcelette, in the latter of which tanks were used for the first time, Thiepval Ridge and the Ancre. By the time the fighting officially ended, British and Dominion dead came to over 95,000. Listed amongst the dead were men from Chichester.

One of the struggles that formed part of the Somme campaign was for the village of Ovillers on 7 July. Four men from Chichester died in that attempt. They were Privates Alec Oliver Ayling, Archibald Frost and Lawrence McCaul and Lance Corporal Harold Thomas Burchett Richardson.

Meanwhile, back in Chichester, as men from Sussex were dying in the fields of France, the Chichester Primitive Methodist Church held a garden fête and sale of work at the home of Mr and Mrs

Men going over the top.

Hutton. The fête was to raise funds for the repair of the chapel roof in Broyle Road. Over £50 was raised. Another garden fête, this time organised by the Mayor and his wife, took place on 13 July to collect funds for the French Red Cross and on this occasion £93 6s 2d was raised.

In August, a further seven Chichester men lost their lives on the battlefield. They included two, Private Thomas Brookes and Private Ernest Turner, who died from the wounds they suffered in battle.

On Saturday 5 August an inquest was held in Chichester into the death of a farm labourer, John Leggatt of East Wittering. Leggatt had been driving a wagonette containing two calves down College Lane when a loud crash was heard. People going to investigate found Leggatt pinned underneath the vehicle, which had overturned. George Ransome, who was nearby, tried to get Mr Leggatt out and a passer-by held the horse steady so that it would not drag the cart along, thus causing more injury to the stricken man. Leggatt was still alive but died five days later in hospital. Witnesses said they believed that something had caused the horse to shy. A verdict of accidental death was returned.

Another terrible accident occurred on 3 August when a 17 year old youth from the city, Laurence Horton, was drowned at Chidham whilst trying to rescue two youngsters who were in difficulties in the water. Laurence had been sitting on the bank of the river with Lillie Heaps when he heard cries for help. Despite being diabetic and in poor health himself, Horton dived into the water to help. One of the youngsters managed to pull himself to the bank and Horton assisted the other into a rowing boat in the middle of the river. Then as Horton tried to swim back to the bank a current took him under. His body was recovered later and buried at Chichester on 15 August.

In September another fifteen Chichester men lost their lives in the war. Many of these died on the Somme, including Private Thomas Webb, of 13 Washington Street; Corporal George Edward Knight, of 58 Broyle Road; and Private Maurice Botting, of 85 North Street.

Another view of British soldiers attacking the German lines.

October saw another fourteen Chichester men die in the war. These included Corporal Cecil Ralph Ansell, who was the brother of William Albert Charles Ansell, killed in action on 12 August 1915, thus leaving their parents, living at 76 Spitalfields Lane, to mourn a second son. In the same month the Bishop of Chichester moved from his Palace to a smaller residence in response to a joint appeal from the National War Savings Committee and the Board of Trade for householders to cut down on their use of coal.

In November, the fighting on the Somme officially came to an end, but not before another seven Chichester men had perished. One of those killed was Private Frederick Hill, one of the group who were fined on 17 March for refusing to report for duty after being conscripted. He died on 8 November, leaving his parents, William and Agnes of 19 St James' Road, Portfield, to mourn him.

On 21 November a concert was held in South Street by members of the Royal Army Medical Corps to raise funds so that Christmas presents could be sent out to the 'boys in khaki' who were serving their King and country. At about the same time, scaffolding was put around The Cross due to a recent storm that had loosened the ball on top. A council spokesman stated that repairing it would not be a big job.

On 2 December, Fanny Hawkes, the wife of the publican in charge of the Castle Inn on The Hornet, was fined £1 for selling beer outside hours. Inspector Brett and Sergeant Evans saw a man named Barnes enter the premises at 6.25 am. The two police officers followed Barnes into the pub and found Barnes drinking beer. The landlord, John Hawkes, was not on the premises at the time but his wife, who had served Barnes, was found guilty and ordered to pay the fine at five shillings per week.

Another court case was heard on 9 December when William Sharp was summoned for aggravated assault on his wife, Annie. On 24 November, Annie had spent the morning working on mangling clothing she had just washed. She intended to do the same in the afternoon but for some reason William took exception to this and punched her on the shoulder. This was not the first time William had appeared in court for similar offences and, as a result, he was sentenced to three months imprisonment with hard labour.

The last month of the year saw three more Chichester soldiers die, the last being Private Alfred Faith, of 61 Orchard Street, who was killed in action on 20 December. His death meant that in 1916 more than eighty men from the town had given their lives for King and country.

CHAPTER 6

The Royal Sussex Regiment

The men from Chichester who joined the army and subsequently lost their lives fought in many different regiments and corps. Some, for example, joined the Hampshire Regiment or the Machine Gun Corps or, later still, the Tank Regiment; a great many joined their local regiment, the Royal Sussex.

Of all the men of Chichester killed in action or who died from wounds or other causes, around 40 per cent were with the Royal Sussex Regiment. These men fought in almost every theatre of war and the regiment as a whole were the recipients of 69 battle honours including four Victoria Crosses. The Royal Sussex was divided into a number of battalions, many of them formed after Lord Kitchener had made his appeal for a million men. The various battalions of the Royal Sussex Regiment in the war were:

1st Battalion
At the outbreak of war in 1914 they were in Peshawar and remained in India throughout the war.

2nd Battalion
They began the war based in Woking but were sent to France at the outbreak of hostilities. They fought in various actions,

Men of the Royal Sussex Regiment.

including Mons, the Battle of the Marne, First Ypres, Aubers, Loos and Flers-Courcelette.

3rd (Reserve) Battalion
They were in Chichester in August 1914 and remained in England throughout the war. After war was declared they were moved to Dover and then, in May 1915, to Newhaven, where they formed the garrison there.

1/4th Battalion
In Horsham at the start of the war, but were moved to Cambridge in the spring of 1915 and in May 1915 to Bedford. On 9 August 1915 they landed at Suvla Bay as part of the Gallipoli campaign and in which they suffered heavy casualties. They then fought in Palestine, including at the Second and Third Battles of Gaza. The battalion moved to

France in May 1918 and saw further action, including fighting at Ypres.

1/5th (Cinque Ports) Battalion
Based at Hastings in the first months of the war and landed in France in early 1915. They fought in various actions on the Western Front including Albert, Polygon Wood and Poelcappelle. In November 1917, as part of the 48th Division, they moved to Italy, where they saw further action, including the Battle of Vittoria Veneto.

1/6th (Cyclist) Battalion
Based in Brighton in August 1914 but almost immediately after the outbreak of the war moved to Norfolk. The battalion remained in the United Kingdom throughout the war, moving to St Leonard's, then Folkestone and then Wingham in Kent. In the summer of 1918 they were sent to Ireland.

2/4th and 2/5th (Cinque Ports) Battalions
Formed in the period November 1914 to January 1915. The battalions underwent various name changes and spent the duration of the war in England.

2/6th (Cyclist) Battalion
Formed at Brighton in November 1914. In 1916 they were sent to India but in late 1918 were despatched to Vladivostock (in Russia) as part of the force sent to fight against the Bolsheviks. They returned to England in November 1919.

3/4th and 3/5th Battalions
Formed in 1915 as home service units.

3/6th (Cyclist) Battalion
Formed in 1916 but was soon absorbed into a new, reserve battalion.

15th Battalion

Formed on 1 January 1917 and remained in England throughout the war being stationed first at Bedford, then at Ipswich and finally near Cambridge.

16th (Sussex Yeomanry) Battalion

Formed in Egypt on 3 January 1917 from dismounted Sussex Yeomanry. They saw action at the Second and Third Battles of Gaza and the capture of Jerusalem. Transferred to France in May 1918, they were involved in further fighting, including action in the Somme region.

7th (Service) Battalion

Formed at Chichester on 12 August 1914 in response to the appeals from Kitchener. It landed in France on 1 June 1915. Fought in such battles as Loos, Albert, Pozières, Cambrai, Bapaume, Amiens and the Battle of the St Quentin Canal

8th (Service) Battalion (Pioneers)

Formed at Chichester in September 1914 and then moved to Colchester. After moving to Salisbury Plain for training, they landed in France in July 1915, where they were in action at Albert, Bazentin Ridge, Delville Wood, Thiepval Ridge, Pilkem Ridge, Passchendaele, Amiens and Bapaume.

9th (Service) Battalion

As with the 8th Battalion, they were formed at Chichester in September 1914. They moved to Shoreham in April 1915 and landed in France on 1 September 1915. They saw action at Loos, Delville Wood, Guillemont, Vimy Ridge, Messines, Pilkem Ridge, and Cambrai.

10th (Reserve) Battalion

Formed in October 1914 and moved to Colchester in spring 1915. They moved to Shoreham on 1 September 1916; they never left the UK.

Soldiers of the 8th Battalion, Royal Sussex Regiment. This battalion fought on the Western Front at famous places on the Somme, such as Delville Wood and Thiepval Ridge and at Third Ypres.

More men from the 8th Battalion.

11th (Service) Battalion (1st South Down)
Formed on 7 September 1914 and moved to Maidstone in July 1915. They landed in France in March 1916, where they fought at Richebourg l'Avoué, Ancre, Thiepval Ridge, Pilkem Ridge, Polygon Wood, Passchendaele and Bapaume. Returned to Britain in June 1918 and reorganized, it went to Russia in October 1918.

12th (Service) Battalion (2nd South Down)
Formed on 3 November 1914 and moved to Maidstone in July 1915. They landed in France in March 1916 as part of the 39th Division. The battalion was disbanded, as part of the reorganization of the BEF, in February 1918.

Officers and NCOs of the 12th Battalion, Royal Sussex Regiment, one of the battalions informally known as Lowther's Lambs.

13th (Service) Battalion (3rd South Down)
Formed on 20 November 1914. Moved to Maidstone they were sent to Aldershot in September 1915. They landed in France in March 1916, where they fought at Richebourg l'Avoué, Pilkem Ridge, Polygon Wood, Passchendaele and Bapaume. The battalion was disbanded in August 1918.

14th (Reserve) Battalion
Formed in August 1915. It ceased to exist in September 1916, having never left the UK.

17th Battalion
Formed in France in May 1918, they were involved in a number of actions including the Battle of Albert and the Final Advance in Artois and Flanders.

51st (Graduated) Battalion
A training unit based at Colchester.

52nd (Graduated) Battalion
Another training unit based at Colchester.

53rd (Young Soldier) Battalion
A basic recruit training unit based at Aldershot.

For further information about the formations and actions in which the various battalions of the Regiment were involved, visit the excellent website developed by Chris Baker, the Long, Long Trail: www.1914-1918.net.

The four recipients of the Victoria Cross from the Royal Sussex Regiment were:

Sergeant Harry Wells of the 2nd Battalion – at Le Rutoire on 25 September 1915

Lieutenant Eric McNair of the 9th Battalion – at Hooge, in Belgium, on 14 February 1916

Company Sergeant Major Nelson Carter of the 12th Battalion – at Richebourg l'Avoué on 30 June 1916

Lieutenant Colonel Dudley Johnson of the 2nd Battalion – at the Sambre-Oise Canal on 4 November 1918

CHAPTER 7

No End in Sight – January to April 1917

Despite the war, 1917 began with an ancient Chichester tradition. On the first day of the year, men from the city gathered at the Cross and marched around it singing Auld Lang Syne. This was followed by a rousing rendition of the National Anthem.

Later on the 1st there was a motor accident at the same spot. An army vehicle, driven by Sergeant Albert Badge was travelling from west to east. At the same time, a taxi, driven by Mr A T Prescott was travelling from north to south and the two vehicles met at the Cross. The subsequent collision sent Sergeant Badge's vehicle into Lennards' shop and did considerable damage.

This event had consequences, for on Saturday 13 January Sergeant Badge appeared in court. Constable Langley was the first officer on the scene and found that the sergeant did not have a driving licence. As a result, Sergeant Badge was fined £2.

On Monday 8 January, a doctor was called to 35 Westgate to attend to 86-year-old Phoebe Louisa Leggatt, who had fallen down the stairs in the early hours of the morning. Dr Burrell found the old lady sitting in an armchair, apparently still in good health. Told that she should go back to bed, Mrs Leggatt playfully replied that she would do so on condition the doctor gave her a bottle of brandy. The next morning, 9 January, when a neighbour checked on Mrs

Leggatt, however, she found that she had died during the night. The inquest, on 10 January, returned a verdict of accidental death.

A terrible tragedy took place on Sunday 14 January at a farmhouse at Donnington, a couple of miles south of Chichester. Guy Homer was the 15-year-old son of the head of the household, Frank Homer. Father and son had spent the morning walking the fields with a shotgun, which they used to scare off birds from their land. They returned home for lunch and, after they had eaten, Guy said that he was going to go back outside and do some more shooting. Taking the gun, he sat down in an armchair, broke the weapon open, put in a shell and closed the gun. Despite his finger being nowhere near the trigger, the gun went off and the shot struck his seven-year-old niece, Vera Wells, who was sitting just in front of him, playing with her toys on the floor. The shot passed through Vera's head, exiting close to her left eye and killing her instantly. The inquest, four days later, returned a verdict of accidental death and, despite Guy being cleared off all blame, the young boy was very distraught and expressed the wish that it had been he who had perished.

On 26 January, the newspapers reported the death of Private William Chase, who was killed on 16 December 1916. William, who lived at 52 St Pancras, was part of a working party when a German shell burst amongst them. It was reported that William had left a wife and two young children. In January only one Chichester soldier met his death; Sergeant Frederick Bunce of the Machine Gun Corps died in hospital at Rouen from wounds that he had received.

On Saturday 3 February a tragic accident took place at Hunston. A number of schoolboys from Chichester had ventured out to the canal and decided to test the ice by walking on it. One boy, 11-year-old William Barber, of 33 Tower Street, walked out further than his friends and on to ice that was much thinner. The ice gave way and William fell into the freezing water. By the time help had been summoned it was too late and William had drowned. At the inquest, held on 6 February, a complaint was made that the body of the child had not been treated with due respect. William had been put onto a rough cart and only partly covered with a ragged sack. The police explained that this was all that was available; but the Coroner stressed that the dead should always be treated with care and respect as they were moved to the mortuary.

In February, six more Chichester men were killed in the war. One of these was Private Wilfred Tee, the second of the men who were fined in March 1916 for failing to report to the army after being conscripted. He was killed in action on 21 February. Another life lost was that of Trimmer George Scutt, who served on board the trawler *Evadne*, which had been converted for use as a minesweeper. The ship struck a mine on 27 February.

Another inquest involving a drowning took place on 28 February. It was held at the City Club in North Pallant and concerned the death of 72-year-old Miss Helen Purchase, whose body was found in the Lavant the previous Friday. She had only recently moved from Theatre Lane to Basin Road and was apparently a happy enough soul. On the day in question, however, she was seen walking towards the Lavant by a group of schoolboys who were playing football on a nearby field. Her body was later recovered from the river by Constable Charles Ellis, who found her handbag on the bank close by. The inquest failed to discover how Miss Purchase had come to be in the water and was unable to say whether this was suicide or an accident. A simple verdict of 'found drowned' was therefore returned.

On 10 March Rupert Burch appeared in court charged with riding a cycle without lights. Normally such an offence would have incurred a fine of five shillings or so but the circumstances of this case were somewhat different. Mr Burch's attention was called to his offence by Constable Woodley, who shouted out that he had not got a light on his bicycle. To this Burch shouted back; 'Yes, I know I haven't; good night Mister Woodley.' That cheek meant that Burch was fined £1 instead.

On 4 April the death was reported of Private Frank Cutten, who was a well-known local footballer and athlete before the war. Frank played for Fulham Reserves and was promoted to the first team in the season of 1906–07. He was killed in an attack on the German trenches on the morning of 23 February and left a wife, Anetta, and a young child.

It must be remembered that although many Chichester soldiers lost their lives in the war, many others suffered terrible injuries but nevertheless survived. One such case was that of Private E.H. Squibb of 25 Franklin Place. On 25 April, his relatives received a letter from a comrade, Sergeant Frederick Pyle, stating that Squibb had been hit in the face by a bullet whilst fighting in Egypt and consequently had lost his left eye.

CHAPTER 8

The Grinding Battle Continues – May to December 1917

April saw two major events: the entry of the United States into the war and a new allied offensive on the Western Front.

The Americans finally went to war on 6 April for a variety of reasons, ranging from anti-German feeling after the sinking of the *Lusitania* in 1915 and outrage over the Zimmermann Telegram, which incited the Mexican government to attack the USA. The British intercepted the cable and passed it to the Americans in mid-February. This, combined with the opening of an unrestricted submarine campaign by the Germans, was enough to sway the American Congress to support a declaration of war, which happened on 6 April. The effect was largely a morale one at first; it took some months to recruit, train and equip a huge new army. The major military contribution was to come in the final months of the war; but the strategic impact of the consequence of the entry of the United States into the conflict was immediate.

The second major event was the opening of the Battle of Arras on 9 April. Initially it was very successful and the British and Dominion troops made substantial gains. However, the Germans steadied the line. Haig felt compelled to support the disastrous

French offensive (the trigger for the 'mutinies' in the French army) and prolong the offensive. There was a higher daily casualty rate than the Somme; the offensive officially ended on 16 May.

On 2 May the local newspaper reported the death of Flight Sergeant W.E. Stidolph, a Chichester athlete, who was a member of the Royal Flying Corps. He was killed in an accident whilst testing an aircraft at Farnborough. Witnesses reported that the machine had dived suddenly whilst making a turn.

Another death reported in May had a more tenuous link to the city. In January Corporal J. Culver married a Chichester girl, Miss N. Morgan, of 7 Franklin Place. Since that date, Corporal Culver had been awarded the Military Medal but now his death was reported. He was killed in action on 13 April after just three months of marriage.

One of the famous employers in Chichester was the Shippam's meat paste factory. Over a hundred of the company's staff answered the call to arms when Kitchener had asked for a million men to join up. Twelve of those employees would lose their lives in the fighting; one of them was Private Harry Shepherd, who died in May in hospital in France of wounds received on 23 April. He was the second son lost by Mrs Shepherd, of 108 Grove Road; another, Arthur, was killed in action in August 1916. Mrs Shepherd had a third son still serving in France.

The arrest of three men in May on charges of stealing petrol made headline news in May. Thomas William Ford, a tradesman from Southgate, William Harley, the licensee of the Unicorn Inn in Eastgate and postman Percy Charles Lucas, of 27 Chapel Street, were accused of the theft of four cans of petrol, each holding two gallons. Inspector Brett informed the magistrates that he had been keeping watch on Percy Lucas and had seen him remove the cans at 5.30 am on 16 May. These had been driven away in a Post Office sidecar and handed over to the other two men. All three were sent for trial at the next assizes, which opened in July; only Lucas was remanded in custody, the other two men receiving bail.

On 7 June, a major limited offensive took place along the

Eastgate, with the Union Inn at the centre of the picture. The landlord, William Harley, was one of the men accused of stealing petrol in May 1917.

Messines Ridge, south of Ypres. This battle, launched by the firing of nineteen huge mines, was a prelude to a planned larger attack. The 'prelude' lasted for seven days and cost the Allies almost 25,000 men – but also cost the Germans an approximately similar number and achieved its objectives.

On 18 July, a massive bombardment of the German lines in the Salient opened, signalling the first phase of the Battle of Third Ypres for which Messines had been the prelude. The battle became better known by the name of the village where the final phases of the fighting were fought out in the most appalling conditions: Passchendaele.

Empire Day took place on Thursday 22 May when the sun blazed from a clear blue sky. Over 1,500 attended the event in Priory Park, as did a large number of wounded soldiers from the local hospitals. At the end of the day the British flag was unfurled and saluted and then the National Anthem was sung.

Saturday 2 June saw a curious incident at Chichester railway station. At around 7.15 pm, Mrs Mary Ann Hector, who was aged

66 and lived at Bosham, ran to catch a train. In fact, the train in the station was not the one she wanted and a very breathless Mrs Hector then took a seat on one of the station benches. A few moments later she fell from the bench and collapsed onto the platform. Doctor Buckell was called but by the time he arrived Mrs Hector had died. Her husband later reported that she had been rather ill for some time.

On 20 June the death of Private Alfred John Welcome, the son of Mr and Mrs Welcome, of 50 Orchard Street, was reported. Serving in the Royal Fusiliers, Alfred was wounded on 7 June and died two days later, on the 9th. He was a married man but had no children. The death was also reported of Private Arthur Hollist, of 67 Whyke Lane. He was in the Royal West Kent Regiment but was acting as a stretcher bearer when he was killed on 7 June.

The first military death in July was that of Harry William Miles of the Royal Marine Light Infantry. He was aboard HMS *Vanguard* at Scapa Flow when, just before midnight on 9 July, the ship exploded. It was believed that the cause of the disaster was a fire that heated cordite near an adjacent bulkhead. There were only two survivors and Harry was one of 804 men killed.

It was also in July that the petrol stealing case was heard at Lewes. Despite the police evidence, Thomas William Ford, William Harley and Percy Charles Lucas were all adjudged to be not guilty and walked from court free men. More Chichester men were killed in action during the month, including Private Francis Ralph Wickenden. He was the second son lost by William and Alice Wickenden, of 9 St Martin's Street, losing another son, George, at Loos on 25 September 1915.

There was tragedy too for Mr and Mrs Smith, of 189 Oving Road, Portfield; before the war they had two sons. The first of these, Lance Corporal Thomas George Smith, was killed in action on 16 November 1916. Now they received news that their only surviving son, Arthur, who had been serving in France for a year and nine months, had been severely wounded and, as a result, had his left arm amputated.

The news was also bad for William and Sarah Hopkins, of 55

HMS Vanguard *which exploded at Scapa Flow on 9 July 1917, killing Harry William Miles from Chichester.*

East Street. One of their sons, Lance Corporal George Sidney Hopkins, was a member of the Tank Corps. He was severely wounded by flying shrapnel and had both legs amputated. Unfortunately this did not save his life and he died from his wounds on 2 August. George was only 23 years old and was well known in the city as his father, William, was the Superintendant of the Cattle Market.

On 22 August, Mrs Harman, of 2 Buller Villas, The Broadway, Summersdale, received news that her son, Private Richard James Harman, had been killed. He had been out in No-Man's Land with a raiding party and all had returned safely to the British trenches. Richard was just about to enter a dugout when a shell burst close to him and he was killed instantly.

On Monday, 17 September, the citizens of Chichester were treated to a display of flying prowess when, at around 9.00 am, a military aeroplane appeared over the city and executed a number of daring manoeuvres, including rolls, dives and even loops. Many of those watching were sure the craft would crash at any moment and were quite relieved to see it finally straighten out and head off into the distance.

On 26 September Mrs Challen, of 14 The High Street, in Somertown, received two pieces of bad news. One of her sons, Lance Corporal Archibald Greenshields, was killed in action on 8 September by a shell. A second son was badly wounded and was now in hospital in Huddersfield.

What turned out to be quite an amusing incident occurred in the city centre on 3 October. A number of cows belonging to Tom Field were being led down South Street by a farmhand named Challen. Close to The Cross one of the cows decided to take a different turn and lumbered through a plate glass window into the premises of Sykes and Son, drapers. Turning and attempting to get out, the cow then backed into two other windows, showering glass all over the street. Fortunately neither the cow nor any of the shop staff were injured.

The war often demonstrated that a soldier's luck was a fickle mistress. Private Thomas William Budd, of 43 Cavendish Street, was once taken prisoner by the Germans. In the confusion of battle, he managed to slip away from his captors and return to the British lines. His luck ran out, however, on 1 October, when he was in his trench when a mortar bomb landed a few feet away. He was killed instantly. Much the same sort of thing happened the very next day to Private William Glue, of 10 Northgate, who was also killed. He left a wife and five children. William was one of the men from the Shippam's factory who joined up early in the war.

November was another dark month for families in Chichester, with no less than fourteen men being lost at the front. Some of those men died at Ypres but six were lost in the fighting at Gaza in Palestine. They included: George Leach, of 14 Kingsham Road; Arthur Eade, of 164 Orchard Street; Edward Hawkins, of 30 Basin Road; Ronald Sandal Richards, of Somertown; Sefton Charman Baker, of 158 Orchard Street; and Frank William Bacon, of 110 Bognor Road.

THE GRINDING BATTLE CONTINUES

At the beginning of November a serious fire occurred at the premises of Pillow and Lewis in East Street. The main damage was to the rear of numbers 31 and 32 and it took some hours to bring it under control. Damage was estimated at around £2,000.

On the same day in November, Mr and Mrs Welch, of 100 Victoria Road, Portfield received two official pieces of news from the War Office. Opening the first they discovered that their son, Sergeant George Welch of the Royal Sussex Regiment had been awarded the Distinguished Conduct Medal. They then opened the second communication, which stated that their other son, 19-year-old Frederick, had been killed in action on 26 October.

At about the same time, Nellie Blanche Tilley, of 62 Broyle Road, received a communication which told her that her husband, Private Thomas Henry Tilley, had been killed in action on 10 October. Thomas was 26 years old and his wife was pregnant when he went to the front. She had since given birth to twins, who were now four months old. Thomas never saw his children.

A strange incident was reported on 14 December, relating to an event that occurred on the evening of Monday the 12th. A young marine, Arthur James Riley, the son of James Riley, of Caledonian Road, was in his barracks at Eastney. At around 9.10 pm, Arthur went to his room where he read for a while before retiring for the night at 9.50 pm. Lights out was at 10.15 pm and the room, which Arthur shared with other marines, was plunged into darkness. Not long afterwards, Arthur got out of bed and when one of his comrades asked him what he was doing, Arthur replied that he was going to the lavatory. A few minutes later there was a cry from Gunner Higham who was outside, saying that a man had fallen from a window. Going to investigate, Arthur's comrades found his body lying on the ground 30 feet beneath the lavatory window.

There was no suggestion that Arthur had taken his own life. He was described as a jovial chap, well liked by his fellow marines. It was possible that he had opened the window either to get some fresh air or perhaps to have a crafty cigarette and leaned forward just a little too far. A verdict of accidental death was returned by the inquest.

In December reports were published detailing the death of another soldier who had, before the war, been a promising footballer. Private Albert Smithers, of 18 St Paul's Road, was taking rations up to the front line when a shell exploded close to him, killing him outright. Albert was 27 years old when he died on 6 November and was a great loss to his parents, George and Elizabeth.

On Saturday, 15 December, a 16-year-old youth, Thomas Hall, of Tower Street, appeared before the magistrates on a charge of firing a catapult in St Paul's Road. Special Constable Hopkins saw Hall with another boy at 6.45 pm on 10 December. Both boys had catapults and were firing stones in all directions, with no regard for any injury or damage that they might cause. Hopkins managed to seize Hall but the other boy ran away. Hall refused to name him and, it being rather dark at the time, Constable Hopkins was unable to identify him.

Normally such an offence would result in a small fine but Hall was something of a recidivist and this was his third appearance in court in 1917. On 25 January he had been fined £3 for stealing sugar and on 16 November £2 for stealing a large ham. For the second offence he also received a sentence of twelve months' probation. Since he was now in breach of that order, the magistrate felt that he had no option but to send Hall to prison in the hope that this might shock him into realising that his behaviour was unacceptable. Consequently, Thomas Hall received a sentence of 14 days.

December saw seven Chichester men killed whilst serving their country. The very last death of the year was that of Private Francis Cecil Dewey, who was killed in action on 31 December. It brought the number of Chichester men who had made the ultimate sacrifice in 1917 to around eighty.

The year had been one of hopes raised only to be dashed – the best example of which was the November Battle of Cambrai; marking the first use of massed tanks. The year had added hundreds of thousands to the casualty rolls of the conflict, with neither side really gaining the upper hand, but rather a constant slog of tired army against tired army. The Bolshevik revolutions in Russia resulted in the signing of an armistice on 16 December. Thus there was little real hope at home at the end of 1917 that the bloody conflict would end any time soon.

CHAPTER 9

No End in Sight – January to March 1918

The year 1918 opened with a horrific accident in Chichester. Amelia Fanny Green was busy doing various household chores in her home at 22 Grove Road. Her 21-month-old daughter, Phyllis Eileen, was happily sitting on a chair in the front room whilst her mother went about her work. A heavy fireguard stood in front of the roaring fire.

At one stage, Amelia had to go outside to hang some washing up in the garden. She was only outside for a few minutes and during that time she heard no noise or cries of distress from inside her house. When she returned, however, she saw to her horror that the fireguard was lying on its side and Phyllis was in the fireplace, her clothing on fire. The poor child never cried or screamed and Amelia did all she could to save her daughter, badly burning her hands in the process. The doctor was summoned and the baby rushed to hospital but it was all to no avail and Phyllis died at 6.45 pm that evening.

The first Chichester military casualty of the year was Leading Seaman Alfred Charles Young, of 28 Bognor Road.

Alfred was serving on HMS *Opal* and had been on that ship at Jutland which soon afterwards returned to her normal duty of minesweeping. On 12 January 1918 the *Opal*, along with HMS *Narborough* and HMS *Boadicea*, were involved in a night patrol,

HMS Opal, *on which Alfred Charles Young of Chichester died when the ship ran on to rocks in January 1918.*

seeking German ships believed to be laying mines off the coast of Scotland. Once again the weather was appalling and *Boadicea* ordered the other two ships back to Scapa Flow. On the way back the two ships ran onto rocks in a snowstorm. Only one man survived from both wrecks, and a total of 188 lives were lost.

On Saturday 19 January, 15-year-old Jack Tupper was working at a printing works in St Johns' Street when he caught his right hand in one of the machines. The top of one finger was cut off and another finger was badly crushed. The accident was all the more unfortunate because Jack was an accomplished pianist and had accompanied many concerts in the city.

On 29 January, Fanny Beaumont, of 39 Whyke Lane, received news that her husband, Private James Arthur Beaumont of the Royal Army Service Corps, had been killed in action on 21 January. Fanny was left to cope alone with her seven children.

On 6 February an amusing case was heard before the Chichester magistrates. George Pearce was charged with being drunk in North Street on Sunday, 3 February. George had been so incapable that the officer who arrested him had to take him to the police station on a handcart. Asked to explain how he had got into such a state, George replied that he had been unable to get any beer and had been forced to drink whisky, which he was not used to. He was fined the maximum of ten shillings.

Another military death was reported on 20 February. Robert Ernest Keast Hodge was born in Chichester and lived at 27 Caledonian Road with his parents, Henry and Mary. He worked for Barclays Bank in the city but decided that he wished to make a new life for himself in New Zealand so, at the age of 20, he left Britain and set up on the other side of the world. As soon as war was declared in 1914, Robert tried to join the New Zealand Army. Unfortunately, he was turned down as he suffered from varicose veins. Determined to do his bit for his country, Robert had medical treatment and was then accepted into the army. He served first in Egypt and then was sent to France. By 1918 he had reached the rank of Company Quartermaster Sergeant but was killed in action at Polygon Wood on 5 February, which happened to be his 30th birthday. He and two other men were killed when a shell exploded above them.

Two other serving Chichester men lost their lives in February 1918. The first was Private Arthur William Edwards, of 11 Whyke Lane, who was killed on 8 February. The other was Private Edgar Jarman, of The Laurels, 23 Cleveland Road, who died on 16 February whilst a prisoner in German hands.

The second week of March was Aeroplane Week in Chichester and funds were raised to help the Royal Flying Corps. It was a most successful event and the marvellous sum of £72,000 was collected, chiefly through the sale of raffle tickets for a cash prize of £75.

On 19 March, Private William Ayling, of 23 The Hornet, died from wounds he had received when hit by shrapnel. Despite the fact that he was only 19 when he died, William had already been awarded the Military Medal for bravery on 21 July 1917.

Up to this point, March had been a relatively quiet month on the battlefields of France. In the period from the beginning of March until 20 March, four Chichester men had lost their lives, the last of whom was Private Ayling. Things were, however, about to change.

For some considerable time there had been little movement on the Western Front but the German authorities knew that now that America was in the war it would only be a matter of time before huge numbers of fresh troops would be facing them in France and Belgium. They decided that now it was a matter of determined effort to force an end to the war, helped by the ending of hostilities on the Russian Front.

So it was that on 21 March 1918, a massive German offensive opened up with the aim of dividing the British and French armies. The offensive was codenamed Operation Michael and it was a partial success. The Germans advanced many miles and the British and French suffered very heavy casualties and had to withdraw over the devastated terrain of the old Somme battlefields. However, the German attack failed before Arras and failed to divide the allied armies – and the ground captured was largely a desert of devastated land.

Having suffered just four men lost in early March, Chichester lost a further seven of her sons in the rest of the month. The last of these was Major Denys Huntingford Hammonds, the son the Reverend and Mrs Hammonds, of 37 North Street. Major Hammonds was killed on 30 March.

Operation Michael would last until early April; there would be worse to come.

CHAPTER 10

The Great German Offensives – April to July 1918

On the first day of April, the citizens of Chichester were surprised to hear the Cathedral Clock strike eight at 7.45am. It was later explained that this was an April Fool's joke.

Meanwhile, in France, the German offensive of Operation Michael ended on 5 April with the capture of over 1,200 square miles of territory from the Allied forces. During that time, two more men from Chichester were killed in action. The first of these was Private Arthur Cecil Croxford, of 100 Bognor Road, who died on 2 April; Lance Corporal Leonard Arthur William Dancer, of 30 Caledonian Road, lost his life on 3 April.

Just four days after the first offensive of 1918 had ended, a second one began. Operation Georgette began on 9 April and this time the intention was to attack the British lines in Flanders. Yet again the number of casualties was very high and much more territory was lost.

On 7 April, a terrible accident took place in the skies near Chichester. Two aeroplanes had set off from a nearby airfield. One was piloted by Second Lieutenant Norman Herbert England, who was instructing a pupil, Clifford Hackman. The second plane was piloted by Victor Raleigh Craigie.

At 1.15 pm, having finished his instruction, England was coming in to land when the other plane got too close and Hackman's wing clipped England's tail. Both craft now spun out of control and plunged into the ground, killing all three men.

A most interesting notice appeared in the Chichester newspapers on 10 April. A large block of print proclaimed that in 1917 the county of Sussex produced 26,600 tons of potatoes but had, during the same period, consumed 58,900 tons thus leaving a deficit of 32,300 tons. The notice then appealed for all citizens who had farms, allotment and even small gardens to grow more potatoes so that the county may eventually become self supporting.

In France, things were now so desperate that on 11 April, Field Marshal Sir Douglas Haig issued what became known as his 'Backs to the Wall' message to all British troops. It read: 'Three weeks ago today the enemy began his terrific attacks against us on a fifty-mile front. His objects are to separate us from the French, to take the Channel Ports and destroy the British Army.

'In spite of throwing already 106 Divisions into the battle and enduring the most reckless sacrifice of human life, he has as yet made little progress towards his goals.

'We owe this to the determined fighting and self-sacrifice of our troops. Words fail me to express the admiration that I feel for the splendid resistance offered by all ranks of our Army under the most trying circumstances.

'Many amongst us now are tired. To those I would say that Victory will belong to the side which holds out the longest. The French Army is moving rapidly and in great force to our support.

'There is no other course open to us but to fight it out. Every position must be held to the last man: there must be no retirement. With our backs to the wall and believing in the justice of our cause each one of us must fight on to the end. The safety of our homes and the freedom of mankind alike depend upon the conduct of each one of us at this critical moment.'

On 24 April an inquest opened in Chichester. Private Richard Lang, a native of Preston in Lancashire, was serving in France when he was wounded in his left hand. Sent back to England to recover, Lang was sent to Graylingwell where he made such a rapid recovery that he was informed that he would soon be discharged and then sent back to the front line. Lang was distressed at the thought of having to go back to the trenches so, on 17 April, he went into the toilets and cut his throat with a razor. He was found half-an-hour later lying dead in a pool of blood.

On 29 April, Operation Georgette ended. During the period of this second offensive, thirteen more Chichester soldiers were killed. One month later, on 27 May, yet another German offensive opened. This third attack was codenamed Operation Bluche-Yorck and was concentrated against the French. This operation would last until early June and was yet another German success.

It was also in May that the people of Chichester were delighted to hear that the Duke of Richmond had kindly decided to offer Priory Park as a gift to the city to be used as a war memorial for those who had fallen. For many years the park had been held on a lease by the Priory Park Society but now, once the details were finalised, the area would be freely available for the people of the city to use.

On 9 June, a fourth German offensive opened. This operation was directed against the French lines south of Verdun, and given the code-name Operation Gneisenau. Once again a great deal of territory was lost to the Germans but, even as they retreated, the French took many prisoners and some of these soldiers expressed the view that Germany was spent and these offensives could not continue much longer

Still the citizens of Chichester were firm in their determination. On 12 June a letter appeared in the *Chichester Observer*. Written by Mr W. Elderton, of Cavendish Street, it asked readers if they knew of a more patriotic street than the one he lived in. He remarked that there was a roll of honour outside number four and that, despite the street only having some 50 houses, the families there had sent no less than seventy-two men to the forces. Two families had sent five sons, two more had sent four, five had sent three and eight had sent two. Seven of those men had already lost their lives fighting for their country and seventeen had been wounded, some more than once. One man was missing, presumed dead, and another was a prisoner in Germany. In fact, though of course he could not know it at the time, Mr Elderton would see his street lose two more men before the war was over.

On 15 July, the fifth German offensive of the year opened. This too was aimed mainly at the French lines but, unlike the other four operations, this did not result in a massive German advance. This time the attack was unsuccessful and it was the French who advanced. This fifth offensive continued until 18 July.

The month of July saw eleven more Chichester soldiers die including four on the same day at Grand Rozoy. These four were: Private Francis Eli Boniface, of 11 Guilden Street; Private George Perry, of 13 South Pallant; Lance Corporal Archibald Charles Shier, of 32 St Pancras; and Lance Corporal William Tabour, of 43 The High Street, Portfield. All four were in the Royal Sussex Regiment and all four were killed in action on 29 July.

CHAPTER 11

The End – August to November 1918

On 7 August one of Chichester's most accomplished soldiers was killed in action. Rowland William Theodore Thorowgood, of 18 Cleveland Road, enlisted in the Royal Warwickshire Regiment in September 1914. By the end of that year he had been promoted to lance corporal and in March 1915 was promoted again to corporal. Just two months later, in May 1915, he was promoted sergeant and then was commissioned on 29 November 1915.

In February 1917 Rowland was wounded in the right leg but was soon back at the front and distinguishing himself in battle. In July he was promoted, to lieutenant and in November 1917, aged 24, was awarded the Military Cross. Now, less than a year later, he had been killed in France, leaving his parents, Arthur and Ethel, to mourn his loss.

The day after Lieutenant Thorowgood died the Allies launched their own massive offensive against the weary Germans. A force of British, Australian, Canadian and French troops attacked on the Somme front. This time it was the Allied forces who advanced and much of the territory that they had lost in the previous months in that sector was recaptured. Not only was the attack a great success, but German troops were surrendering in droves. Surely, now the end was finally in sight.

Still Chichester men were dying in the fighting. On 8 August, the opening day of the Allied offensive, another lieutenant, William Stephen Rousell, of 23 Green Lane, went over the top with his men at 4.00 am in thick fog. He was killed within a few feet of the trench he had just left. The next day, 9 August, Private Edwin Arthur Cumberledge, of 18 Oving Road, was also killed in action.

The Allied advance continued on inexorably into September. On the 29th, the infamous Hindenburg Line suffered a major breach. At this time there were numerous acts of bravery from Sussex soldiers, many of them from the Chichester area. One such man was Private George Sivyer, from 33 Florence Road, Portfield, who was driving an ambulance under heavy fire, taking wounded men to hospital. For his bravery he was awarded the Croix de Geurre by the French. An unassuming George simply posted the medal home to his mother for safekeeping in a letter in which he wrote, 'Thank God I got through without a scratch.'

The Allies were now attacking on all fronts. On 15 September, the British troops in Salonika launched a major attack against the Bulgarians and four days later, on the 19th, the British attacked the Turks at Megiddo. Back in Chichester, people were horrified to hear of a murder within the city.

On Saturday, 21 September, Henry Phillips, of 130 Broyle Road, happened to look over a row of bushes at Barrack Field, Brandyhole Lane, in Summersdale, when he saw what looked like a child's doll. On closer inspection he saw that it was in fact the body of a new born baby.

The police were alerted and Constable Tuckey arrived on the scene and removed the body to White's mortuary in South Pallant. There, Dr A.M. Burford performed a postmortem and later reported to the inquest that the child was born about a week before the body was found and had lived for some thirty hours. The cause of death was a blow to the right side of the head and it did not appear to be the result of an accident. The verdict was one of murder by person or persons unknown; the case was never solved.

Two more Allied attacks took place at the end of September. On the 27th, a major push started at the Canal du Nord and on the 28th an offensive was launched near Ypres. Both attacks saw the Germans retreating again. The next day the German High Command informed the Kaiser that the situation was hopeless and the war was lost. The dire situation was underlined when, on the last day of September, Bulgaria, the first of the Central Powers to capitulate, agreed an armistice with the Allies.

On 1 October, Damascus was captured from Turkish forces and five days later, on 6 October, the first overtures for peace were made by the Germans, who wished to discuss terms. Eight days after this, on 14 October, Turkey requested its own armistice.

In Chichester, on 23 October, an inquest opened into the death of a pedlar, John Collins. He was a traveller who moved around the country making and selling nets and was well known in the city as a regular visitor. Collins returned to Chichester in mid-October and was staying with an old friend, Thomas Ayling. On the fourth night there, Collins said that he felt worse than he ever had in his life before and had to be helped up to bed. At 6.00 am the next morning a loud groan was heard and Mr Ayling went to investigate. Two minutes later, Collins breathed his last and a postmortem, performed by Dr Barford, revealed marked arterial degeneration and a greatly enlarged heart. Death was due to natural causes.

The Central Powers were now in complete disarray. On 27 October, Austria-Hungary sought an armistice and two days later many of the soldiers serving in the German fleet at Wilhelmshaven mutinied, spreading disquiet across the entire country.

On 4 November, the last Chichester soldier to die whilst the war was still raging, was killed in action. He was Private Gilbert Elliott, of 14 Kingsham Road. Serving in the Royal Fusiliers, he left a widow, Alice Maud.

In Chichester, on 6 November, the funeral of Private Alexander Ambrose Jellett, of 48 Orchard Street, took place. He had fought bravely for his country and had come home on six days' leave. Having survived all the horror and destruction in France, he succumbed to the influenza epidemic that was raging across Europe and died at home. He was buried with full military honours, including a firing party and buglers sounding the Last Post.

On 9 November, Kaiser Wilhelm II abdicated and Germany was declared a republic. The following day, the terms of the armistice were given to the German High Command. The thirty-five terms included: that the armistice would be effective six hours after signing; that German troops must be cleared from Belgium, France, and Alsace-Lorraine; that the left bank of the Rhine was to be evacuated; and that the colony of German East Africa was to be surrendered.

The Armistice itself was signed at 5.00 am on Monday, 11 November 1918 and came into effect some six hours later, at 11.00 am. The guns fell silent and the war was effectively finally over.

In Chichester, victory was announced that same Monday. It happened to be Gun Week and a six inch British howitzer had been set up close to the Cross to aid fundraising. That was where the crowds now gathered and at 11.00 am, as the Armistice came into force, the Cathedral bells rang out to loud cheers from the assembled crowd.

At noon, the deputy mayor, Alderman Turnbull, came to the Cross and the National Anthem was sung. This was followed by three cheers for the navy, army and our allies. The streets of Chichester were filled with happy people promenading along the thoroughfares greeting each other and the city did not fall quiet until late into the night.

Two days later, on the evening of Wednesday, 13 November, a service of thanksgiving was held at the Cathedral before a packed congregation. At last, peace had come to the city of Chichester.

CHAPTER 12

Peace

Although the war had ended, Chichester soldiers were still dying; but this time the enemy was influenza.

The first peacetime victim of the epidemic was Lance Sergeant Archibald Cooper, of 210 Oving Road. He died from the disease in Dover Military Hospital three days after the end of hostilities. He had a distinguished military record, which included being awarded the Military Medal at Cambrai in November 1917, where he was badly wounded in the right hand. His body was brought back to Chichester and interred at Portfield Churchyard.

The disease also claimed the lives of the families of soldiers. One such was Private Henry Ide, of 64 High Street, Somerstown. He was blinded in the war and now a cruel fate took his wife Elizabeth and his eldest daughter Gladys within a week. The final military death of the year was that of Private Charles Gobey, of 1 Parchment Street. He died from influenza in hospital in France on 18 December. His brother, Thomas, had been killed in action just over a year earlier, on 4 October 1917.

More than 300 Chichester men had lost their lives fighting in the war but it was now time to build the peace and part of that was the formation of a new government that would lead Britain into this new era. A General Election was called but this would be rather different to previous elections.

The major change came in February 1918, when the

Representation of the People's Act received Royal assent. This Act meant that now all men over the age of 21 were eligible to vote; however, even more significant, women over 30 could also vote. There had, of course, been campaigns led by the suffragettes to give women the vote but the new law was largely the result of the vital part women had played in the war effort.

The General Election took place on 14 December and the poll saw a decisive swing towards the Coalition parties, who won 459 of the 707 seats available. In Chichester, it was a straight fight between Lord Edmund Talbot, the Conservative Unionist candidate, who had been the member for the city since 1894, and the Labour candidate, Frederick Ernest Green. When the result was declared, Lord Talbot had received 14,491 votes as against 6,705 for Mr Green.

Lord Edmund Talbot, the Member of Parliament for Chichester throughout the war and who was successful again at the General Election of 1918.

On the day after the General Election, a strange coincidence with echoes of 1914 occurred. The war had, of course, started with the assassination of the Archduke and now, as it ended, a curious parallel took place. On 15 December, Major Sidonio Paes, the Portugese President, was travelling to Lisbon's railway station to take a train to Oporto when a man stepped out from the crowd and shot him three times. Mr Paes died at the scene but his killer fared little better, for he was seized by the onlookers and lynched on the spot.

The new year of 1919 dawned, the first peaceful one since 1914. One of the earliest reports in the Chichester newspapers was of the death of one of its oldest citizens. At midnight on 2 January, Mrs Parrington, who was aged 101 and who had been living with her son, the Reverend J.W. Parrington, at St Bartholemew's vicarage, passed away. She had first arrived in the city as a new bride in 1847.

On 7 January, over 200 children were treated to a fancy dress dance at the Assembly Rooms. A variety of costumes were seen and prizes awarded for the best boy and girl of ten years and under and the best boy and girl over ten. After the prizes were awarded a photograph was taken and the children then entertained by a band.

The Assembly Rooms were also used for a most important meeting on 4 February. Presided over by the Mayor, the discussion concerned the erection of a war memorial to commemorate those who had fallen. It was decided that a representative committee would be formed to decide what form the monument should take. All agreed that it must be a fitting monument to those who had died and an inspiring symbol to those who would come after.

Although the war was over, men from Chichester who had served in the forces were still becoming casualties. The dreadful influenza outbreak still claimed lives and in the early part of 1919 there were three such deaths, one each from the army, navy and air force. On 18 February, Private First Class Archibald Cosens of the Royal Air Force died at his home, 34 George Street. Just two days later, on 20 February, Leading Stoker Charles Alfred May, of 34 Basin Road, also passed away and on 21 February, Private Walter George Dew, of 37 Tower Street, followed them to the grave.

Some of the institutions set up to help the war effort were now closed down as they were no longer needed. On 14 February the Women War Workers establishment in West Street was formally closed down at a meeting at which thanks were given for the sterling efforts the women had provided. On the 26th, the National Egg Collecting Depot, which had served wounded soldiers so well since January 1915, was also closed.

At the end of February, the Bishop of Chichester announced his retirement which would take effect on 1 May. He had served as the city's bishop for just over eleven years.

It seemed that despite Britain now being at peace, it would be some time before people forgave Germany. At the beginning of March, Dr Read, the conductor of the Chichester Musical Society, announced that he had banned German music.

In April, St George's Day, Wednesday 23 April, saw a most solemn service at the cathedral. The event, which began at 3.30 pm, was a commemoration service for all the men from Sussex who had fallen in the war. The Bishop was given the names of the 6,800 men who had given their lives and the lists were placed solemnly on the altar. The colours of the Royal Sussex Regiment, in which many of the men had served, were then placed inside the cathedral. Admission to the event was by ticket only, as it was expected that the number who wished to attend would be many more than the cathedral could hold. First consideration was given to those who had suffered a bereavement. It was, after all, a service for the people. The Royal Sussex Regiment had distinguished itself many times during the years 1914 to 1918 and men from the regiment served in almost every theatre of the war, earning a total of four Victoria Crosses. Some time after the commemoration St George's Chapel in the cathedral was dedicated as a memorial to the men of the regiment who had died.

Although many organisations established during the war were now closing, others were just opening up for business. Perhaps one

St George's Chapel in Chichester Cathedral, dedicated to the Royal Sussex Regiment.

of the most important opened when the Dean of Chichester presided over a meeting in the Assembly Rooms, which witnessed the establishment of a branch of the League of Nations Union. There was an excellent turnout despite the weather being rather bad and many of the people there expressed delight that this new international body would certainly be able to do much to prevent any future war as terrible as the one that they had just endured.

Those who supported this new group could not know, of course, that history has a habit of repeating itself.

The official dedication of the Chichester War Memorial to the Fallen, in March 1920.

Index

Battles:
  Arras, 71
  Aubers Ridge, 35
  Cambrai, 78, 93
  Gallipoli, 33, 36, 39, 60
  Jutland, 46, 48–50, 81
  Loos, 39–40, 42, 44–6, 62, 74
  Mons, 21, 60
  Neuve Chapelle, 31
  Passchendaele, 73
  Somme, 50–1, 53–7, 72, 84, 89
  Ypres, 25, 31–3, 46, 60, 73, 76, 91
Bishop Otter College, 16
British Expeditionary Force (BEF), 21, 39–40

Cavell, Edith, 40–1
Chichester Cathedral, 8, 14, 40, 50, 85, 92, 96–7
Chichester Cross, 41, 56, 67, 76, 92
Chichester Observer, 48, 87
Chichester Station, 15, 35, 73
Council House, 10, 44

Ferdinand, Archduke Franz, 17, 19–20

Garland, Mayor, 10, 14, 27, 44, 54, 95
Graylingwell Hospital, 31–2, 35–6, 38, 43, 50, 87

Kaiser Wilhelm II, 18, 91–2
Kitchener, FM Earl, 48, 50, 72

Portfield, 35, 50, 56, 74, 77, 88, 90, 93
Princip, Gavrilo, 17, 20
Priory Park, 16, 73, 87

Public Houses:
  Arundel Arms, 13
  Blacksmith's Arms, 13
  Castle Inn, 13, 38, 56
  Dolphin, 11
  Good Intent, 13
  Plough and Harrow, 13
  Prince Arthur, 13
  Prince of Wales, 13
  Royal Oak, 11

The Globe, 12
Unicorn Inn, 72–3

Royal Sussex Regiment, 21, 23, 35, 36, 38, 44–6, 51, 59–66, 77, 88, 96–7
Royal West Sussex Hospital, 11–12, 37, 50

Sarajevo, 17, 19–20
Scapa Flow, 48, 74–5, 82

Ships:
HMS *Aboukir*, 22
HMS *Black Prince*, 48–9
HMS *Boadicea*, 81–2
HMS *Bulwark*, 26–7, 50
HMS *Cressy*, 22
HMS *Good Hope*, 26
HMS *Hampshire*, 48, 50
HMS *Hogue*, 22–3
HMS *Indefatigable*, 48, 50
HMS *Invincible*, 48
HMS *Monmouth*, 26
HMS *Narborough*, 81
HMS *Opal*, 81–2
HMS *Queen Mary*, 48–9
HMS *Vanguard*, 74, 75
HMS *Viknor*, 29
RMS *Lusitania*, 33–4, 71
Shippam's, 9, 72, 76
St Richard's Church, 38

Streets:
Adelaide Road, 42

Basin Road, 76, 95
Bognor Road, 39, 76, 81, 85
Broyle Road, 44, 54–5, 77, 90
Caledonian Road, 77, 83, 85
Cavendish Street, 13, 76, 87
Chapel Road, 38
Chapel Street, 72
Cleveland Road, 83, 89
College Lane, 54
Cross Street, 12
East Street, 11, 14, 29, 30, 41, 75, 77
East Walls, 35
Eastgate, 72–3
Eastgate Square, 38
Eastgate Street, 13
Ettrick Road, 41
Franklin Place, 30, 70, 72
George Street, 13, 35, 95
Green Lane, 90
Grove Road, 72, 81
Guilden Street, 88
Kingsham Road, 76, 91
Lion Street, 27
Little London, 13
North Street, 11, 25–6, 83–4
Northgate, 76
Orchard Street, 57, 74, 76, 91
Oving Road, 41, 90, 93
Parchment Street, 35, 93
Russell Street, 44
South Street, 10, 12, 16, 24, 35, 37, 41, 56, 76
Southgate, 72

INDEX 101

Spitalfields Lane, 56
St John's Street, 24, 41, 82
St Martin's Street, 74
St Pancras, 13, 25, 35, 68, 88
St Paul's Road, 78
The Hornet, 11, 13, 23, 38, 41, 56, 83
Theatre Lane, 69
Tower Street, 13, 24, 35, 68, 78, 96
Washington Street, 22, 55

West Street, 11, 14, 16, 21, 96
Westgate, 67
Westhampnett Road, 22, 38
Whyke Lane, 39, 49, 74, 82–3
York Road, 22, 39

Victoria Cross, 59, 65–6, 96

War Office, 29, 31